AN ORDINARY ADVENTURE

Retracing Mom and Grandpa's 1934 trip on Route 66 - in a Model A!

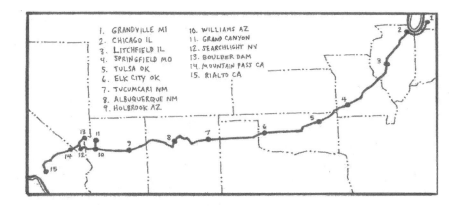

1. GRANDVILLE MI
2. CHICAGO IL
3. LITCHFIELD IL
4. SPRINGFIELD MO
5. TULSA OK
6. ELK CITY OK
7. TUCUMCARI NM
8. ALBUQUERQUE NM
9. HOLBROOK AZ
10. WILLIAMS AZ
11. GRAND CANYON
12. SEARCHLIGHT NV
13. BOULDER DAM
14. MOUNTAIN PASS CA
15. RIALTO CA

DIANE WOOD

May all your journeys be joyful !

Diane Wood

Published by:

Life In The Dash

11278 Los Alamitos Blvd, #132

Los Alamitos, CA 90720

First Printing, 2018

Printed in the United States of America

ISBN: 978-1718694798

Dedication

To the people in my life who have made it all worthwhile:

Gerald Gaughen, my husband for more years than I'm willing to admit; for always supporting me in my endeavors and challenging me to think things through, and for being the willing and unpaid chauffeur on this journey.

Brendan, my beloved son and gift from God; for giving me the wonderful experience of being a mother, and for completing the PhD dissertation that sparked this whole undertaking.

Keith, my older brother, who is the keeper of the family memories and my "research assistant" - he remembered things in our family history that I was unaware of because I was too young.

Bob, my faithful father, who was always there, and in 1934 watched the love of his heart set off into the unknown with his future father-in-law.

Isaac, my Grandpa, who lived with us until I was 9 years old. I wish I could have gotten to know him as an adult and heard the stories first-hand.

Vi, my Mom, who loved me and always listened, and had the good sense to keep a journal of this trip with my grandfather.

and...

Betsy, my brother's wife, my "sister" and Mom's "daughter," who didn't live to be a part of our trip, but who was with us in spirit and for whom the car is named.
She loved a good time!

Without them, there would be no book.

About The Author

Diane has worn many hats throughout her various careers. After graduating from the University of Michigan with Bachelor's and Master's degrees, her first career was teaching public school in California, both middle school and high school – math, history and English. After hitting the magic number of 13, she decided it was time to move on.

After a bad experience in the stock market following the advice of a broker, she decided there were probably many other women like her – intelligent, but ignorant about how the markets worked. So, being an experienced teacher, she figured she could teach them. But she better educate herself first, so she acquired the professional designation of Certified Financial Planner. She ran her own office helping people to prepare for and thrive financially in retirement. But after 24 years, it was time to move on again.

Before she exited the financial planning field, her interest in the Bible had led to her second Master's degree at Biola University. Even before she graduated, she was teaching Bible classes and speaking at her own and other churches. So for over 16 years, concurrent with her professional life and afterwards, she was teaching again – just in a different field.

The death of Diane's father when she was 26 (and he only 59) sparked an interest in health and nutrition which flowered over the years with certifications in Emotional Freedom Technique and HeartMath, and then led to her becoming a Certified Health Coach and Functional Diagnostic Nutrition Practitioner.

With all this varied background, you may wonder how this helps her in writing a memoir recreating a trip that took place before she was born. The answer is – not all of it, except she's literate in her native language and loves her family, history and road trips!

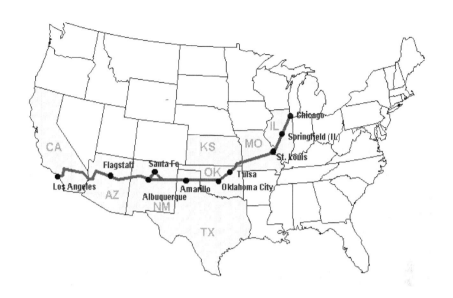

Route 66

from

Chicago, Illinois

to

Santa Monica, California

November 11, 1926 – June 27, 1985

...but still, it lives!

TABLE OF CONTENTS

Introduction 1

PART ONE PREPARATION 6

Chapter 1 - Finding the Car 7

Chapter 2 - In The Shop 11

Chapter 3 - Learning to Drive 16

Chapter 4 - Betsy's Bustle 20

Chapter 5 - The Itinerary 23

PART TWO THE TRIP 26

Chapter 6 - Nostalgia 27

Chapter 7 - The Three Angels 31

Chapter 8 - Rain, Rain, Go Away! 36

Grandville MI to Chicago IL 1934 36

Grandville MI to Chicago IL 2017 38

Chapter 9 - The World Comes to Dwight 44

Chicago IL to Litchfield IL 1934 44

Chicago IL to Litchfield IL 2017 48

Chapter 10 - Betsy Is A Star! 52

Litchfield IL to Springfield MO 1934 52

Litchfield IL to Springfield MO 2017 54

Chapter 11 - The Last Original Road 62

Springfield MO to Tulsa OK 1934 62

Springfield MO to Tulsa OK 2017 64

Chapter 12 - Red Dirt and Bible Study 69

Tulsa OK to Elk City OK 1934 69

Tulsa OK to Elk City OK 2017 70

Chapter 13 - From Midwest to Southwest **74**

Elk City OK to Tucumcari NM 1934 74

Elk City OK to Tucumcari NM 2017 76

Chapter 14 - Our Spanish Heritage **84**

Tucumcari NM to Albuquerque NM (2 days) 1934 84

Tucumcari NM to Albuquerque NM (1 day) 2017 86

Chapter 15 - Wide Open Spaces **93**

Albuquerque NM to Holbrook AZ 1934 93

Albuquerque NM to Holbrook AZ 2017 94

Chapter 16 - Preservation **101**

Holbrook AZ to Williams AZ 1934 101

Holbrook AZ to Williams AZ 2017 103

Chapter 17 - The Grandest Canyon **107**

Williams to the Grand Canyon and Back 1934 107

Williams to the Grand Canyon and Back 2017 108

Chapter 18 - Over The River **113**

Williams AZ to Searchlight NV 1934 113

Williams to Boulder City 2017 117

Chapter 19 - Dam! That's Big! **119**

Searchlight NV to Mountain Pass CA via Boulder Dam 1934 119

Boulder City and Boulder Dam 2017 122

Chapter 20 - At Last! **126**

Mountain Pass CA to Rialto CA & Uncle Joe's House 1934 126

Boulder City to Rialto and Home 2017 (2 days) 128

PART THREE EPILOGUE **131**

Chapter 21 - *Wait! There's More!* **132**

Chapter 22 - Going Home...139

Chapter 23 - Don't Ever Leave Me Again!............................145

Postlude...147

Acknowledgements..148

It was the beginning of an ordinary adventure, undertaken by ordinary folks, but one that would be remembered because Mom was a bookkeeper and very meticulous about keeping track of things. She got out her little notebook and before Grandpa started the car, wrote:

10-28-34 – Sunday Mileage 49901. Left home 9:50 A.M.

Home was Grandville, Michigan, Mom (Viola) was my mother and Grandpa (Isaac or Ike) was my grandfather. The Van Koevering family had its roots back in the Netherlands; in fact, my grandmother, Ada (Adrianna) was born there. Grandpa was the son of a Dutch immigrant.

Many of the Dutch settled in western Michigan, the area around Grand Rapids, Zeeland and – no surprise here – Holland. My grandpa's father had emigrated from the Netherlands in 1847 at the age of six; like so many other immigrants, his family was looking for a better life. Isaac was born the eldest of eight children in 1867, two years after the end of the Civil War.

So where does the story behind this adventure begin? It begins with the death of my grandmother Ada on Independence Day that summer. Grandpa's two younger brothers, Joe and Martin, who lived in California, decided it would be good for him to pay them a visit and get away from home for a while.

Well, the older kids were not sure that was a good idea! (My mother was the youngest of seven.) After all, Grandpa was 67 years old and he'd be travelling alone, and he wasn't that good a driver. So Mom, being the youngest and single, was "elected" to drive with Grandpa on this journey of a lifetime. She was 24 at the time and serious about Bob, whom she would marry the next June. Whatever objections Bob may have had about this crazy idea he kept to himself.

The stage was now set for an Ordinary Adventure. But what makes this an adventure? As a former English teacher, I had to do what I would have advised my students to do – look it up! What I learned from the American Heritage Dictionary is this: *An unusual experience or course of events marked by excitement and suspense.* This trip held the promise of both. I can imagine that Mom especially might be excited. She had never been more than a few hundred miles from home in her entire 24 years. The suspense might be obvious; what could go wrong? Would they have car problems? Would they get sick? Would the people they met be friendly? Where would they stay? I don't really know what their expectations were, but they were travelling in hard times.

It was 1934 – five years into the Great Depression. One fourth of the work force was unemployed. Grandpa and Ada knew families who had lost their homes and farms to foreclosure. During the 1930s, some 2.5 million people left the Plains states to get out of the Dust Bowl, a great number heading in the same direction as Mom and Grandpa – west to the Golden State of California. It was a desperate time for many people.

There was even talk of changing our system of government to overcome this crisis. Charles Lindbergh spoke admiringly of the Nazi regime in Germany after a visit there and a budding Communist party was growing in the United States. President Franklin Roosevelt had only been in office a little over a year and the full impact of the New Deal was yet in the future.

Even though unemployment was high, Mom and Grandpa had fairly good jobs. Since 1922, Grandpa had been a valuable and well-respected employee of the American Seating Company in Grand Rapids and had worked there as a draftsman and pattern maker. Many years later, he even won recognition in the Company newsletter for having developed "a mechanical robot, used throughout the nation to illustrate good posture principles. He was highly regarded as a mechanic in both wood and metal." Evidently, he had the full support of the company for taking a leave for a few months. Mom worked at the Blue Valley Creamery as a bookkeeper and was given a two-month leave. Her boss was supportive enough to contact a friend in Chicago, where they stayed for three nights while visiting the World's Fair.

So amidst all this economic and political uncertainty, a 67-year-old man and his 24-year-old daughter set off to drive from Michigan to California in a Model A on Route 66, which wouldn't be fully paved for another three years! Perhaps this would assuage the loss they felt over Ada's passing. Thus they set off.

When Mom moved to California in 1984 to be closer to us and we saw her more often, she didn't talk too much about the trip, even though she still had the little notebook, carefully saved in a box. It had been 50 years before and maybe she had forgotten some of the details. I don't remember when or why I got the idea, but I copied each page of her notebook and asked her to type up some comments next to her handwritten notes. At the time, she was living independently and still had her old Smith-Corona typewriter, so she set to work. (The typing awards she won in Business College came in handy here.) Then the notebook and the commentary went back in the box for a few more years.

It was just a few years after she passed on in 2003 when I ran across Mom's little notebook again, but I didn't think too much about it then. Outside of sentimental value, what interest could there be in something so seemingly insignificant as this notebook measuring 3¾ by 5¾ inches? It was over 75 years old and getting kind of fragile, so I kept it in a file titled "Grand Rapids to Pasadena" along with a few old maps she had saved. It was a nice remembrance of my mother and I didn't want to lose it. Why I gave the file that label, I can't say. Was there a premonition of a future trip, even back in 2003?

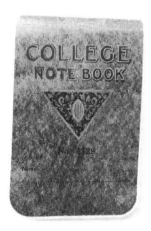

The Notebook

The next time the notebook saw the light of day was after my brother Keith and I met in London in 2008 to celebrate his 70th birthday. We had a marvelous time because we share many of the same interests. After I got home, I thought it might be fun if he and I retraced Mom and Grandpa's trip. But it didn't tweak his interest at that time, maybe because he was facing two knee replacements. The notebook stayed in the file.

Then, a few years later, our son Brendan was preparing his doctoral dissertation at the University of Texas and asked to borrow the little notebook. He wanted to see if there was any first-hand information he could use in his research. After he returned it, back in the file it went where it slumbered undisturbed until 2016.

The next step in this saga may be a God thing. After Brendan finished his dissertation and because I asked, he presented me with the one and only bound copy. (Pause here for a few moments of motherly pride!) Reading the first chapter detailing how the creation of the Lincoln Highway influenced (and still influences) our culture, I saw how his thesis, the influence of *place* in our culture and our personal experiences, was summed up in the phrase "......knowing where we've been is an important factor in knowing who we are."

Then the thought came to me: What did Mom and Grandpa experience on their trip? I began to wonder again what it would be like to follow in their tire tracks and try to share in that experience. It was then I said to myself, "Drat! I'm not getting any younger. It's now or never."

I must have mentioned it more than once to my long-suffering husband, Gerald, who also wasn't getting any younger, and who agreed it would be a great idea. "*BUT,*" he said, "*it's not authentic if we don't do it in a Model A!*" Somehow, that had never crossed my mind.

So, I appointed him the "car guy" to see how far this would go. Well, it went all the way. He searched for hours, if not weeks, to find the perfect Model A and he hit a winner. There were some upgrades we made, but basically she is as noisy and smelly as the car Mom and Grandpa drove 2825 miles on Route 66 to California more than 80 years ago.

This is their story – and ours.

PART ONE
PREPARATION

Once Gerald uttered his now-infamous line, *"But it's not authentic unless we do it in a Model A,"* our next task was to find a Model A. There were 4,858,644 of them manufactured from late 1927 through early 1932; just over four years of production, but what a run! It is estimated that around 300,000 of them are still alive somewhere in the U.S. They may not be in the best of condition, so we had to carefully look for one that could take us from our starting point in Grand Rapids, Michigan, back to our home in California.

Since I'm not a judge of car flesh, Gerald undertook, willingly I might add, the task of finding *our* car. Every night after dinner, he'd head to the computer and start searching. He found a nice one in Pennsylvania that was at a dealership. I pointed out the difficulties, not to mention the expense, of buying a car that was out of state, having it shipped to us and getting it properly licensed. It didn't make sense, because then we'd have to ship it to our starting point in Grand Rapids. So I encouraged him to look for something in California.

A nice one showed up not too far from where we live, so we wanted to take a look at it. We sent a request to the owner, but never got a response. So the search went on.

A few weeks later, he got a lead on a good-looking Model A that lived in Escondido, only 75 miles from our home. This time the owner responded when we left a message about wanting to see the car. On a beautiful southern California Saturday, we made the trip to his home where the Model A lived. And she was a beauty!

There had been a body-off-frame restoration some years in the past. Gerald later found out that even the insides of the wheel wells had been painted and the underside had been powder-coated and painted. The upholstery had all been redone too. It looked to be in really great shape. We

The Good-looking Model A

weren't prepared to just write a check and drive it away, so we made arrangements to come back for the actual purchase. We drove home to decide if we really wanted to go through with this.

We decided to go for it, so we contacted the owner and arranged a visit to buy the car and get it home. He was very hospitable and told us about the car. He knew of the history back to 2013 when the car sold at a Barrett-Jackson auction in Scottsdale, AZ. (That was also the year that they sold the 1966 Batmobile #1 for a mere $4,620,000!) For those who aren't familiar with Barrett-Jackson, the company is one of the leading auctioneers of collectible cars in the country. Most, if not all, of the proceeds of some of these spectacular sales are donated to charities. Our car was certainly not one of the top sales, but it still brought a good price. The couple that bought it had fun with it until health issues made it advisable to sell the car.

It was then purchased by an elderly gentleman, a friend of the current owner, who soon realized that the cramped quarters of the driver's side made it nearly impossible to get his feet into the proper position to work the pedals. The owner took him on a test drive to see if he could help and realized it would be a nice car to own for his family. He made an offer and the elderly gentleman accepted.

The new owner made some repairs and used the car on local roads, but realized that routine driving on the highways was not prudent without adding an overdrive. He didn't want to put that much money into the car, so decided that selling was the best option. And that's how we came to be the fourth owners in four years.

Our transaction complete, we arranged for the owner and Gerald to drive the car to our son and daughter-in-law's house in Encinitas and I would follow in my car – a very reliable and easy-to-drive Toyota Camry.

The owner showed Gerald what needed to be done to get it started, the choke-starter-accelerator-throttle-spark advance/retard-clutch shuffle and the quirks it had and they headed off down the road. Then half way to Encinitas, he pulled off to the side of the road and they traded places. This was the true test! Could Gerald drive it the rest of the way without making any serious blunders?

All three of us heaved a sigh of relief when we reached our destination successfully. We joined our family for lunch and then Gerald and I drove the owner back home – in the Camry.

Now we had to get the Model A home. Gerald was not at all sure it would handle the freeway driving that we would have to do, especially without an overdrive. He figured discretion was the better part of valor, so we had the car transported home.

Thus it was that on February 20, 2017, we became the proud parents of a 1931 Ford Model A Victoria. Now Grandpa was frugal enough that he never would have shelled out the money for a Victoria (near the top of the line). Since I have never seen any pictures of their car, I don't know what type it was, but Mom said it was a Model A of some sort.

Since this was such a classic car, we couldn't just keep calling it "the car." It had to have a name. This wasn't an issue while we were busy getting all the fix-up work done, but later on, when we actually got on the road, it seemed like "the car" was a part of the family. It was like a relative who had come to stay with us and would be with us for the entire trip.

But what was a suitable name? Driving somewhere in Illinois, it came to me that "Betsy" would be the perfect name. Why? You only ask that question because you've never met Betsy, my sister-in-law. It's said that opposites attract and that was true with my brother Keith and Betsy. He has always been the well-organized, exacting one. Maybe that comes from being a career Army officer. But Betsy was towards the other end of the spectrum; just a little messy and ever fun-loving. She had a great sense of humor and we had many laughs over the years. Sadly, she passed away in 2011 and never had the chance to be a participant in our trip planning. So how could we not name our car Betsy in her honor? She did do the trip with us from the heavenly realm, as did Mom and Grandpa. It truly was a family endeavor.

We knew from the beginning that Betsy wasn't totally up to snuff for driving on modern highways. Remember, this is still a stock four-cylinder, 40 horsepower machine. Gerald felt it was at least necessary to have radial tires for safety and an overdrive to achieve something more than 40 miles an hour on the freeway. There was more work to be done.

Since we were new Model A owners, we didn't know anyone who could do the work that needed to be done. But the now-former owner had told us about a few people who worked on Model As who could help us do the upgrades that were needed. From there, we got introduced to more and more of the Model A community, and found it to be very active, helpful and well-connected. So one by one, we took steps to get Betsy fixed up. One of the first orders of business was to install an overdrive so our top speed could safely exceed 40 or 45 miles an hour. We knew we'd have to drive some modern highways and Interstates because a substantial portion of Route 66 just isn't there anymore, or if it is, it's not drivable.

We were also told that Model As are notorious for having steering that has a mind of its own. So another upgrade would be to replace the original steering box. And then there were the tires, which looked very nice, but were also quite worn. The list kept getting longer and longer. I began to wonder if the cost of the upgrades was going to exceed the price of the car! Fortunately, that hasn't been the case - at least not so far.

Gerald, now the Chief Car Guy, decided to start with the overdrive. Well, you don't just hop on over to your local Ford dealer to have them install a new overdrive. All these new parts had to be ordered from companies who specialize in the Model A. We found five of them; Bratton's, Snyder's, Mac's, C. W. Moss and Mitchell. The first four have internet and printed catalogues with hundreds, if not thousands of parts. Mitchell is done by phone order. When you call, you are most likely to be talking to Sue Mitchell herself, still running the company her late husband Glenn started in

1978. It seems everyone in the Model A community knows Sue Mitchell.

I became Chief Procurement Officer in charge of part ordering, so I called Sue and ordered the overdrive. She said we could get delivery in about six weeks. That wasn't a problem because we had plenty of other work that needed to be done in the meantime. I had to chuckle, however, when the order receipt arrived in the mail; it had obviously been created on a manual typewriter. Well, the old ways still work!

The former owner had recommended another Model A restorer who referred us to someone who could install the overdrive for us; Tom Endy. When we contacted him, he told us to bring the car over to his house and he could check her out. When we arrived, it was obvious that he had worked on many cars, including his own Model A Victoria. He had a very well-stocked garage with lots of tools and parts, so we felt confident the job would be done right. Since Sue Mitchell knew Tom, we made arrangements for the overdrive to be shipped directly to his house.

Which upgrade should we do in the meantime? It seemed wise to look under the hood and see what needed to be done there. Tom recommended a fellow mechanic who could do just about anything on the innards of a Model A, Jim Nichols. I found it interesting that both of these fellows were retired Boeing engineers and were both in their eighties. I guess retired engineers don't fade away, they just work on Model As!

It wasn't just big stuff we had to buy; there was a lot of small stuff too, right down to the powder-coated black cup holder (to the tune of $51.75!) that Gerald installed. You don't realize how many amenities modern cars have that we all take for granted, like seat belts (Betsy had after-market lap belts), air conditioning (roll down the window), cup holders (hold the cup between your legs), stereo systems (sing loud) and good shock absorbers (bring a pillow).

Here's an example of "stuff" from one of the catalogues that the Chief Car Guy thought we needed:

PART #	QTY	DESCRIPTION	$	TOTAL $
12370	1	BLK WATER PUMP COVER	7.M	7.65
12932	1	GAS TANK NECK EXTENSION	37.95	37.95
12970	1	GAS CAP GASKET	1.10	1.10
23321	1	HOSE GROMMET	1.40	1.40
23340	1	WIPER MOTOR REBUILD KIT	9.50	9.50
23450	1	WIPER BLADE	2.50	2.50
23650	1	WIPER HOSE	3.00	3.00
25080	1	METAL TOOL BOX	195.00	195.00
26331	1	GAS TANK PROTECTOR	11.75	11.75
26332	1	REGISTRATION HOLDER	9.25	9.25
4520	1	TIE ROD END, RIGHT	19.50	19.50
4530	1	TIE ROD END, LEFT	19.50	19.50
4540	1	TIE ROD END BOLTS	4.95	4.95
5571	1	SHORTENED PITMAN ARM	37.55	37.55
5610	1	PITMAN ARM BOLT	2.95	2.95
9521	3	ZOO PLUS OIL ADDITIVE	8.65	25.95
6490	3	600W OIL	10.30	30.90
23310	1	VAC WIPER MTG SCREWS	1.15	1.15
23320	1	WIPER SHAFT NUT	1.20	1.20

The Needed "Stuff"

As Chief Procurement Officer, I set out to enter this order online. Fortunately, I only had to enter the part number and the rest filled itself in. I don't know how many items we eventually ordered, but the stack of receipts is over half an inch thick. Some of these parts were needed as stand-alone parts and some were necessary for completing repairs.

During all this part-ordering, we got an email from Tom that our car was all fitted out with her new overdrive. When we picked her up, he told us that there were actually three of them on the job: Bryan Thompson, Larry McKinney and Tom. Our payment was going to be donated to the Model A Youth Restoration program. We felt good, knowing that we had supported a program that helps young people learn skills restoring Model As. It was a win-win.

Our next upgrade was the tires. They certainly looked pretty, as you can see from the picture in the previous chapter when we first saw the car. But on closer inspection, the treads failed the Lincoln penny test. For those who don't know, the way to see if your tires need to be replaced is to insert a penny with Lincoln's head pointing into the groove of the

The Penny Test

tread. If you can see the top of his head, it's time for new tires. We were overdue. So that brought us to the next hero in our referral network, Nate Jones of Cowboy Tires. He and his son, Nate Jr., and his crew did a great job, not only on the tires, but a number of other things that needed to be done.

From the beginning of April until the end of September with a few breaks in between, our dowager lady was being gussied up for her impending trip of a lifetime by either Tom Endy, Jim Nichols or Nate Jones and Nate Jr. How fortunate we were that these men were all knowledgeable, honest and hard-working.

Knowing that Mom and Grandpa left on their trip on October 28, we planned on leaving in late October also. We picked up the car from Nate on September 23 and would need the intervening time for some other improvements and shakedown cruises to make sure everything was in proper working order, not to mention giving Gerald some additional time to get used to driving an 86-year-old car.

September was also the month that we joined the Orange County Model A Ford Club – a very active group of more than 160 Model A lovers that meets regularly 3 times a month for business and social purposes and telling car stories. Also, the former owner had arranged to transfer his unexpired membership in the International Model A Ford Victoria Association. We also joined the Model A Ford Club of America. That meant that we were now members of both the local and national clubs.

More than one person advised us to buy the membership roster of the national Model A Ford Club of America. If we ever got into trouble on our trip, we should call someone in the local area and they would help us, or know someone who could. It wasn't too long before we found an opportunity to put that to the test.

For most of us of a certain age, we remember what it was like learning how to drive a stick shift. Our family owned a Plymouth Valiant, so I had to learn how to drive it. After a few tries, my Dad gave up trying to teach me because I kept killing the engine. I couldn't seem to get the hang of that fine balancing act between clutch and accelerator.

Finally, my brother Keith came to my rescue and patiently coached me again and again until – ta da! – I got it! Gerald, being a guy, I'm sure had no problem with this.

With regard to Mom, I wondered how she seemed to manage driving a Model A so easily. She made no comments in her notebook about having any problems in that area. Then a few years ago, I ran across a collection of memories she had lovingly typed up for the grandkids. And there I found my answer.

When I was 11 years old, Earl (a brother eleven years her senior) *decided to teach me to drive a car. Earl drove a truck and had to take it home at night and park it in a neighbor's barn, so he would let me sit in front of him and steer it. Then he taught me to use the spark and gas levers and then the brakes.*

He was so tall that I could sit in front of him and he could still reach the pedals. The gas and spark levers were on the steering shaft, just below the steering wheel.

The seats were not moveable then. Also the early cars did not have a door next to the driver – he had to get in and out on the other side. They had to be cranked to get them started. Later, at about the time I started to drive, they had self-starters.

As I read on, I realized I must have never completely read this part of Mom's memories before, because I don't ever remember hearing about what she wrote next.

In the Fall of 1923, when I was 13, my Dad and Art (another brother) and a young fellow friend of Art's went to California. Dad's two youngest brothers lived there and he hadn't seen them in years...Mother and I were alone for a couple of months. Anyway, she would want to go places and I'd have to take her, although I couldn't get my driver's license until I was 14. So she'd put a big pillow under me so that I would not only look bigger, but would be able to see over the steering wheel, and a couple of pillows behind me so that I could reach the pedals, and we'd take the back roads and I'd drive her anywhere she wanted to go.

Earl and Art had MADE me take tires off the rims, take the tubes out, determine where the leak was, patch it, put everything back together and pump up the tire by hand, so I KNEW how to do it. I never had to do it again when I had a flat. Some kind sir would always come along and offer to do it for me.

Now I knew why Mom was so comfortable driving a Model A on their trip – she'd been driving for ten years! When she finally did get her license at 14, driver's licenses had only been issued in Michigan since 1919, five years before. Evidently, the roads weren't busy enough in Grandville that anyone really cared whether she had a license or not.

Grandpa, on the other hand, wasn't as good a driver because he was born and grew up way before cars had been invented and didn't learn to drive until much later into adulthood.

Now that we were the proud owners of a Model A, Gerald, being Chief Car Guy, was determined he would learn all the tricks of driving it. He knew how to drive a stick shift from many years ago, but this was a whole different thing. One of the differences was double-clutching, which I'd never even heard of. That means putting in the clutch to get out of one gear, letting it out, and then putting it in again to go into the next gear. That seemed like way too much trouble to me.

Another issue was the wobbly steering. In an email he sent out to the family after our return, he wrote

It makes for constant attention to handling, as there is probably 20 degrees of play in the steering, especially when passed by a semi or box truck (or car for that matter), and you have to plan your stopping (mechanical brakes). My 80 year old eyes NEVER wandered from the road. That was exhausting.

That summer before our trip, whenever Betsy was out of the shop, we'd take her on shake-down cruises. One day we drove her about 100 miles and everything was fine. We only needed to stop at a gas station, because the tank doesn't hold very much gasoline.

Another time, we offered to take a friend on a trip down Pacific Coast Highway to San Clemente, about fifty miles from our home. This was a weekend day in summer and we should have known better. Coming back on Pacific Coast Highway under those conditions was a real workout. The traffic was very heavy and Gerald was shifting about every ten seconds as the traffic backed up for traffic lights. His legs were very tired by the time we got home.

Gerald thought it was a good idea for me to learn how to drive the car, just in case of an emergency. I figured that's why God invented AAA, but it did make some sense. I do know how to drive a stick shift after all, but hadn't done it for nearly forty years.

My first lesson consisted of making sure my feet could reach the pedals. Unlike in Mom's day, 1931 Fords had moveable seats for the driver, but not the passenger. So we got the seat set so I could reach the pedals. The starter button was quite a ways forward on the floor and I could barely reach it. The accelerator was a little closer and the brake and clutch were where they usually are. So far, so good.

The next step was a bit confusing. I knew I had to turn on the key. But what were all these other levers and knobs for? The knob on the right was the choke, which regulated the air flow into the carburetor. On the steering column were two levers, the throttle on the right and the spark advance/retard on the left.

There was also a lever in the center of the steering wheel itself. What was that? Aha! It was for the headlights.

Knowing all this doesn't mean I could just start up and drive away. My lessons actually never got that far. I'm still waiting for lesson two.

Gerald, of course, got his baptism by fire by doing all the driving on our cross-country trip. His comment after we returned: "The model A is about as aerodynamic as a portable toilet or an old time phone booth."

I loved that comment. What a visual description!

Betsy's Bustle

Since Mom and Grandpa were driving a Model A, they had some of the same issues we faced of where to put stuff. Even though our Model A Victoria was one of the top-of-the-line Fords, that didn't mean it had more room. For instance, there was no trunk or rumble seat that some of the other models had, but we did have a back seat. I was bringing a small suitcase and Gerald had a small duffel bag. We were also carrying some snacks for lunch. But what to do with the spare gasoline and oil and tire irons and tarps and radiator water and rags and...well, you get the picture. Some of this is stuff you don't want inside the car, so we had to get creative.

Chief Car Guy solved all these issues by installing a metal box between the radiator and front bumper and a luggage rack on the back with the wicker basket that you see here. Into the front metal box (which had a lock) went the engine oil and additive, the filler attachment for the gas tank, spare tools, paper towels and other miscellany. The back rack carried a spare gas can and a set of tools. But the real star was the wicker basket itself. Never mind that there were important things inside; the view of the basket was what really counted.

My dear friend, Margaret, had given us the Route 66 sign which was the first thing to be installed. Then Gerald added the smaller signs - JPL for Jet Propulsion Laboratory, where he works, and the NASA sign because JPL is contracted with NASA to build marvelous spacecraft. The stick-on *1931 Earth Rover* is a nod to all the Mars rovers that Gerald has worked on; Pathfinder (1997), Spirit and Opportunity (2004) and Curiosity (2012). All of these rovers have added a tremendous amount to our store of knowledge about the red planet as will the Mars 2020 project when it lands. The *California or Bust* stick-on is letting everyone know where we were headed. Betsy's bustle was a real attention-grabber on the roads and Interstates, especially with the truckers and motorcyclists. What's not to like!

Inside the car, we developed a system that worked for the entire trip. On the passenger side back seat, I put my small suitcase. Gerald did the same with his duffel on the driver's side. In the middle, there was room for a small Styrofoam cooler. In the cooler we had a large bag of mixed nuts, apples, bananas, cheese sticks, bottled water and bottled tea. That was as close as we could get to a balanced diet for our lunches that wouldn't require refrigeration. We never stopped for lunch because it would have taken too much time.

Under the removable back seat lay tools, rags and tire irons in case we had to change a tire. On the floor we would stash jackets, hats, a 1-gallon water jug for the radiator, and the box that held the guide books and maps. Since there was no dashboard or glove compartment, the only luxury item in the front was the two-hole cup holder I mentioned before.

Without a glove compartment, did you wonder where we kept the registration and insurance card? Thank goodness, Betsy had side pockets on each of the doors. On Gerald's side we added a plastic zip-top baggie with a pad of paper to record the gas mileage, a calculator and a pen. On my side was another baggie with the registration and insurance card. In addition, we had full-size pictures of Betsy and a copy of the front-page article from our local newspaper that told about our impending trip.

Gerald and friends in the Mars Yard at JPL

But Chief Car Guy also brought along a picture of himself in the Mars Yard at JPL with full-size duplicates of the Mars rovers Pathfinder, Spirit, Opportunity and Curiosity. Note the difference in size of the baby Pathfinder on his right compared to the Curiosity on his left. What a difference fifteen years can make!

Not to be outdone even by himself, he also brought a picture of himself with his personal best record tuna – 260 pounds! He is a man of varied interests – rocket scientist, deep sea fisherman and car guy. When anyone stopped to admire Betsy and ask about our trip, they got an earful <u>and</u> an eyeful too.

Gerald and his record tuna

Planning our itinerary wasn't so difficult; just follow Mom and Grandpa's route as described in Mom's notebook. My brain thinks better in Excel, so I set about creating a spreadsheet that showed day, route and miles for their trip.

DAY	ROUTE	MILES
1	Grandville MI to Chicago IL	166
2 & 3	Chicago World's Fair	n/a
4	Chicago to Litchfield IL	244
5	Litchfield IL to Springfield MO	275
6	Springfield MO to Tulsa OK	216
7	Tulsa OK to Elk City OK	230
8	Elk City OK to Tucumcari NM	264
9	Tucumcari NM to Santa Fe NM	184
10	Santa Fe NM to Albuquerque NM	128
11	Albuquerque NM to Holbrook AZ	260
12	Holbrook AZ to Williams AZ	188
13	Williams AZ to Grand Canyon & return	132
14	Williams AZ to Searchlight NV	206
15	Searchlight NV to Boulder Dam to Mountain Pass CA	153
16	Mountain Pass CA to Rialto CA	179
	Total Miles	**2825**

Pre-1937 Sign

Obviously, we couldn't follow this exactly because the Chicago World's Fair was no more. The cities were all still there, but Route 66 isn't the same. Even during its official lifetime, from its commissioning in 1926 to its official de-commissioning in 1985, it was re-routed many times and in many places. In fact, we found various places where there were two signs; one saying this route was the pre-1937 route and the other was the 1937 – 1942 route. We tried to follow the route that was used in 1934 as closely as we could.

But eventually both of those routes were bypassed or replaced with more modern highways and the "superslabs" – Interstates 55, 44, 40 and 15. At least we had a framework to follow.

Since Gerald still had a real job, we planned our trip around his work responsibilities. After all, someone has to make sure those rovers get to Mars! He had only two weeks of vacation time, so we had our work cut out for us. At this point, my job title shifted from Chief Procurement Officer to Head Trip Planner. Being a very left-brained well-organized person, I am definitely suited for the job, even though I don't like doing it very much.

I knew some things I wanted to see and visit in and around Grand Rapids, my home town, but also Grandville, the suburb of Grand Rapids where my grandparents lived and my mother grew up. So to my spreadsheet I added locations, addresses and phone numbers for people I wanted to visit with during the trip.

Because of circumstances beyond our control, we didn't get to do and see everything on the list. But that provides fodder for the next trip!

PART TWO
THE TRIP

I hadn't been back to my old home town in a few decades. You know how that is – you have to visit the old house, the old school, the old church and the cemetery where your parents and grandparents are buried. That was our original plan, so that's how we spent the first part of Sunday. We left our hotel in our rental car and headed for downtown Grand Rapids.

Veteran's Memorial Park

When the town was laid out many years ago, a central park was set aside that took up a whole city block. It eventually became known as Veteran's Memorial Park, with monuments and memorials to veterans of many wars.

On one side of the park was the Grand Rapids Public Library, which became known as the Ryerson Library. It was originally funded by Andrew Carnegie, and it certainly reflects the architecture of that era. There are many towns across America which still have Carnegie Libraries.

Grand Rapids Public Library

On another side of Vet's Park was First (Park) Congregational Church, or as everyone always called it, Park Church. My parents started attending here when they moved from Grandville to Grand Rapids in 1939 and it's where I was baptized.

Park Church

In the midst of all this culture, I remember in my high school days when the drive around Vet's Park was the best place to go cruising, that is, if you were a guy looking for a little action. When I got my driver's license, I took my Dad's Buick down there once and drove around but I felt very awkward at the time. Cruisin' wasn't my style.

The Old House

We left the downtown area to ride to the west side where we visited the house where my brother and I grew up. If you look carefully, you can see some windows on the second story above the driveway. That was my bedroom. I recall the dog days of summer – a night-time temperature of 85 degrees and 85% humidity - when I would be lying spread-eagled on my bed at night, hoping for a breath of air. Finally, my dad installed a window fan and I thought I'd died and gone to Heaven!

The Old School

A few blocks away was my old school; Harrison Park Elementary and Junior High School. Now it's only an elementary school, but it still looked the same. I found a small plaque on the side of the building that said 1924. I never realized the building was that old!

Mom and Dad's Gravestone

Our next visit was to the cemetery in Grand Rapids where my folks are buried. My Dad died in 1969 and he waited a long time for Mom to join him in 2003. You can see her small marker on the right has not weathered as much as his.

The last part of our nostalgia visit was to the cemetery in Grandville where Grandma and Grandpa are resting. Again you can see quite a long time between the death dates; 1934 and 1952.

Grandpa's Gravestone

Grandma's Gravestone

As we're visiting all the old haunts, I felt such a tie to the past and my ancestors. I don't know why this seems so important, but there is a kind of visceral connection that goes down the generations. I never knew my Grandmother, but I still have memories of Grandpa, even after so many decades. I can also feel that visceral connection with my son in the descending generation. The umbilical cord is never really cut.

Betsy ready to go

In order to retrace Mom and Grandpa's trip, we had to ship Betsy to Grand Rapids, Michigan from our home in California and fly there to meet her. We wanted a closed transport, not only for safety and security purposes, but also to keep Betsy free of dust, dirt and bug splatters. I was unsure about who to contact about this, but Brendan came to my rescue.

One job he had in his twenties was working for a company that delivered vehicles all over the U.S. He checked and found out his former company could not only transport our car, but they also had a storage facility in Grand Rapids. So on October 11, the car transporter showed up in front of our house. It was huge! The driver showed us it already had about ten motorcycles aboard and our car would add to his load. Gerald drove her on to the transporter and we bid farewell to Betsy.

We presumed all was going well because no news is good news, so we've been told. Betsy should have gotten to Grand Rapids no later than the Tuesday before we were going to arrive on Saturday, October 21. We had no word on the car delivery until I called on October 20, the day before we were flying out. I talked to Paul Schultz, the owner of the storage facility, who greeted me with the news, "It won't start."

It seems when Betsy was ready to come off the car transporter, she was totally dead. There was nothing we could do about it until we got to Grand Rapids except speculate about what the problem might be.

We had arranged to rent a car at the Grand Rapids airport when we arrived that Saturday night so we could do our nostalgia touring around Grand Rapids on Sunday, pick up Betsy later that day and then return the rental car. The plan then was to leave for our Route 66 trip on Monday, October 23. Now that plan was up in the air.

The human mind is infinitely creative. I thought of all sorts of scenarios that could happen and none of them were very good. The worst one was that we couldn't get Betsy to run, so we'd have to get her back on the transporter and fly back home! This was by far the worst scenario; all the time, trouble and expense gone for naught. But there was nothing to be done until we got there. We arrived in Grand Rapids Saturday evening and drove to our hotel in our rental car.

After our nostalgia tour on Sunday morning, I called Paul again and he told us to meet him at his house. That was a surprise! He told us the car was too pretty to leave in the open storage area, so he had it delivered to his home and had kept it in his garage. What service! He was our first angel.

When we got there, we found that the battery was stone cold dead – probably because the little dash light had been accidently switched on for 10 days and totally ran the battery down. Paul was kind enough pull his car up next to Betsy so Gerald could hook up jumper cables. While Betsy's battery was charging, Gerald discovered there was something else wrong too – the distributor was malfunctioning.

Gerald had the foresight to pack a spare distributor in Betsy, so when he discovered the shaft was broken on the original distributor, he figured he could just install the new one. But it wasn't as easy as he thought.

There was also a wire that was supposed to be connected to the alternator, but when he touched it to the contact, it sparked. It's not supposed to do that. There were a few other things that weren't as they should be either. What to do?

Being a little desperate, I called our mechanic, Jim Nichols, in California and put him on the speaker on my cell phone so Gerald could talk to him while he stuck his head under the hood to make repairs. Jim was certainly a good sport about being interrupted on a Sunday afternoon, but not being there to see what was going on, diagnosing and instructing remotely was challenging, to say the least.

Gerald finally speculated that Paul's Subaru was putting out too much power through the jumper cables for Betsy's 86-year-old electrical system and both cars might be damaged if he continued. So upon Jim's advice, they agreed to terminate the remote assistance and get local help. Jim was our second angel.

And then the dark cloud moved in and it started to sprinkle, first lightly, and then more heavily.

A Fix-it Job in the Rain

Have you ever tried working on a car when your glasses are sliding down and water is dripping off your nose?

The end result was we still had a car that wouldn't start and we needed some serious help. Fortunately, I had followed the advice of many people we had met when we first got Betsy and I bought the membership roster for the national Model A Ford Club of America. Remember the advice we got? If we ever got into trouble on the road, we should call someone in the local area and either they would help us or they would know someone who could.

The roster was safely in the box where I was keeping the guide books and maps, so I retrieved it and opened it to the Michigan section. There were five names listed in Grand Rapids, so I called the first name in the roster – John and Barb Battjes. A quick phone conversation brought an invitation from John to have the car towed to his house the next day and he would take a look at it.

Betsy Going to Get Fixed

There was nothing else we could do at that moment, so we left Betsy in Paul's front yard and drove our rental car back to our hotel for the night. Monday morning after breakfast at our hotel, we drove back to Paul's house, called AAA and waited for the flat-bed tow truck. The driver loaded Betsy on his flat-bed and headed off with us following in our rental car.

When we got to John and Barb's house, we learned that John is a very handy guy. Some 30 years ago, he built his own house with the help of a contractor. Not only is there the house and the two-stall garage which houses his two favorites but also a four-stall garage for his other cars.

Before he got to work on Betsy, he showed Gerald his two favorite 1930 Ford Model As – a Coupe and a Fordor (yes that is the correct spelling). John had done all the engine and body work, plus the upholstery. I'm no judge of car flesh, but Gerald said these were practically museum-quality!

Meanwhile, John's wife, Barb, invited me into the house and supplied me with a cool glass of water and that day's edition of the Grand Rapids Press, which I hadn't read since I moved away in 1965. She told me she had some errands to run, so rather than spending my time reading the paper, I agreed to accompany her to the grocery store so I could pick up a deli lunch and some snacks for the road we hoped to soon be traveling on.

By the time my little lunch was almost done, Gerald came in the house and announced that not only was the car fixed, but John refused to take any payment! And this after spending 3 ½ hours on it! He told Gerald he just wanted to make sure we had a safe trip. No doubt about who was our third angel. We bid

John and Barb farewell and started off with two cars – Betsy and the rental car.

Our next task was to return the rental car, but because it was still raining, we decided to go back to our hotel, drop off the groceries and regroup. Since I wouldn't be aboard Betsy to navigate, it was easier to return by a known route. Then the trip from the hotel to the airport to return the rental car would involve one left turn and then following the signs. As we're about to do this, I must remind the reader that we have no functioning windshield wiper, it's still raining and it's getting dark.

Somehow I lost Betsy behind me, so I pulled over into a turnout on the airport entrance road and waited. I thought I saw her feeble headlights coming down the road, so I started up again. When I turned into the car rental driveway, I realized Betsy was nowhere in sight. I was a little concerned because Gerald had no cell phone with him, so I was on my own.

I found the proper drop-off area, checked the car in and looked around. Still no Betsy. I walked towards the sign marked EXIT and when I got close, there she was! Oh, joy! I climbed in and off we went back to the hotel for our last night in Grand Rapids.

We were so relieved that our car was once again operational, but this repair job had delayed us one day on our itinerary. Despite that, we were determined to carry on. The next day we would begin following in Mom and Grandpa's tire tracks.

GRANDVILLE MI TO CHICAGO IL 1934

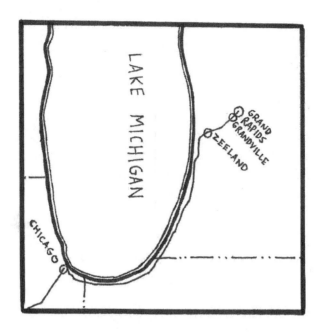

Mom checked her watch – 9:50 am. Grandpa was already in the car as she checked one last time – did she forget anything? The house was all closed up for the few months they would be gone – utilities off, windows shut. She locked the door behind her and got in the car as Grandpa prepared to shift into first, not looking back.

They didn't know what awaited them, but they were prepared. Grandpa had made a box to sit between the front and back seats to hold their dishes, utensils and pots and pans. They were going to cook their own meals in tourist cabins to save a little money. (Grandpa was Dutch, after all. If the Scottish are thrifty, the Dutch are tight!) On the running board were their suitcases and some bedding, just in case the tourist cabins left something to be desired.

Having ridden nearly 3000 miles in our Model A, I figured Mom wasn't writing in her journal while their car was moving. It would have been far too bumpy. So I imagine she wrote in her little journal when they ended that day's travel. Here's how she described their first day:

Weather – dry but cool. Saw car overturned 2 miles west of Hudsonville. Stopped at Cora's house and swiped cupcakes. Stopped at Orin Walbrink's at Ganges.

Saw truck overturned about 3 miles south of South Haven. Arrived in Chicago at 4:30 P.M. Set our watches back one hour to Central Standard Time. Stayed with G. Dekker at 1225 W. 72nd Pl. We're so tired we went to bed about 8 P.M., E.S.T. or 7 P.M., C.S.T.

The Dekker House

The Cora referred to here was Mom's older sister. She and her husband George evidently were at church. They did leave a note, however, so Cora wouldn't think there had been cupcake burglars in the house.

Outside of seeing one car and one truck overturned on the highway, they had an uneventful trip to Chicago. It took over 6½ hours to go 166 miles. Do the math and you'll see that they averaged about 25 miles an hour.

But wait – didn't they stop for lunch or gas or something? Mom, ever the bookkeeper, kept a separate listing of expenses, not only by day, but by category. According to this, they spent 40 cents for lunch somewhere along the way. And that was their exciting first day.

What we thought would be our exciting first day of travel consisted of getting Betsy fixed up so we could hit the road. That means our actual first day of travel was Tuesday, October 24. Since Chicago was only 170 miles or so, we thought we'd have time for a couple of additional stops as long as we were in the area.

Our first stop had been prearranged, delayed and then rearranged. Before we left home, I had spoken with Karen Anderson, a volunteer at the Grandville Museum, about paying a visit. She said she would look through their archives and copy any family records she could find. Fortunately, she was able to change our meeting time from Monday to Tuesday. She was awaiting our arrival.

Although I was born and raised in Grand Rapids, Mom's roots were in the small suburb of Grandville. The family had moved there from Zeeland when she was 5 years old. I had found an old census record on Ancestry.com listing the family home at 7 White Street, so I was excited to see if the old homestead was still there.

About 30 years ago, Mom and my brother Keith and I had done a nostalgia trip and Mom showed us that same house where she had grown up. I recollect a two-story house with a porch in the front. There was a side yard where Mom said the family grew corn and strawberries and tomatoes and other veggies and raised a few chickens. Grandma would send Mom out to the garden to pick a few ears of corn for dinner or some strawberries for strawberry shortcake.

Her least favorite thing was plucking the larvae of the tomato bugs off the plants and dumping them in a can of kerosene. Yuck. She also told us that Grandpa was too soft-hearted to kill the chickens, so Grandma would wring their necks and then everyone would pluck the feathers off so they could have a chicken dinner. This may be more than you ever wanted to know about the "good old days."

On our way to meet Karen, we drove back and forth on White Street looking for the house. Alas, it was no longer standing. Changing times had taken over and many of the houses were now businesses. Ah well...

We drove the few blocks to the Museum and met Karen and another volunteer, Jeanne Beauvais. We were impressed to learn that the volunteers take the second-graders through the museum each year to learn about their small-town heritage. They are hoping in the future to expand the existing square footage and add more exhibits. Virtually all the exhibits have been donated by local residents and I'm sure there are more goodies hiding in basements and attics that would be very welcome in the museum.

Karen & Jeanne at the Museum

Karen and Jeanne did a great job of coming up with many choice tidbits that we were taking with us to look at more carefully later. They found copies of the Grandville City Directory from the 1930s that showed the street addresses where my mom and dad lived. I discovered that sometime between the 1930 census and the publication of the 1937 Grandville City Directory, Grandpa had moved from #7 White Street to #118 and Mom and Dad were living with him. This may have been occasioned by their marriage in 1935.

I realized that these city directories were an earlier version of phone books without phone numbers, but with one added tidbit; they also showed a person's occupation. Sure enough, Mom's occupation was listed as "bookkeeper," Grandpa's was "millwright" and Dad's was "pay roll auditor." All this was fascinating. We wished we had more time to linger, but Chicago was still calling us on. We took a quick tour around the museum and after Betsy posed for a few pictures, we thanked Karen and Jeanne for their help and headed back on the road.

Before Mom and her family moved to Grandville, I mentioned they had lived in Zeeland. Since we were going to pass through Zeeland on our way to Chicago, I thought a stop was in order. One of Grandpa's five brothers, Adrian, whom I always knew as Uncle Ed, had started a local newspaper in town, the Zeeland Record, in 1893. Finding they were still in business, I had contacted the company to see if we could stop by.

I got a response from Kurt Van Koevering, who I calculated was my third cousin, one time removed. He and his brother, Kraig, were now running a full-service graphic printing company, carrying on into the fourth generation. Kurt graciously showed us around and Gerald and I were amazed at the scope of the printing jobs they were capable of doing. Kurt said that originally, the company had to do typesetting letter by letter. Then they graduated to linotype, then electronic and finally digital.

Cousin Kurt

I mentioned to Kurt how unusual it was for a family business to survive into the fourth generation. He showed us the family pictures on the wall, including my Uncle Ed (the middle picture), whom I instantly recognized. I better understood that this company was a matter of family pride and heritage, not just another business.

Kurt had to get back to work so we thanked him for his time and continued on. Our original intent was to follow the route Mom and Grandpa had taken, which would mean taking Michigan Highway 21, connecting with U.S. Highway 31 and thus wending our way to Chicago. We had no problems finding the right highway but after a few miles, Gerald realized Betsy was running kind of rough. Being a fairly rural area, this was not the kind of place we'd like to have car problems. Yes, we had cell coverage to call AAA, but where could we get Betsy towed this time?

We pulled over and Gerald took a peek under the hood and heaved a big sigh of relief. A spark plug wire had become detached from its moorings, so he quickly re-attached it and we were on our way.

As we started up again, we realized this route wasn't going to work. The road we were on only allowed us to go about 30 miles an hour. At that rate, we wouldn't get to Chicago before dark and we couldn't safely drive after dark. Betsy had headlights, but they were so dim they barely lit up the pavement in front of us. So we found the nearest access to Interstate 196 and hustled to our destination.

The distance wasn't the only issue; it was the rain. It had been raining ever since we started. Remember, Betsy didn't have a functioning windshield wiper. We knew we'd have to be very careful on the highways and Interstate freeways considering the poor vision out the front windshield.

Did I mention that the windshield leaked? It was the type of

On the Road to Chicago

windshield that would open out at the bottom to allow ventilation, but this also caused it to leak at the top. Gerald had put Rain-X on the glass, which helped somewhat, but the rain was heavy enough that our vision was obscured all the time.

This picture is only one example of what we faced for nearly 170 miles. The blurry box in the center of the picture is a semi-truck that had just given us a bath with the overspray from its tires.

We had to use our spare rags to lay along the bottom of the windshield to absorb the drips coming from the top where it was leaking. The water would dribble down the inside of the windshield, splash on the little dash rail and then drip on our legs. Even the rags were dripping on us. Every time a large vehicle passed us, we'd get sprayed again, and again...rinse and repeat.

Whenever we stopped for gas or snacks, we'd have to wring out the rags and hope they wouldn't drip on our legs too much before the next stop. By now, you're probably wondering if we were crazy to keep going. But we had a schedule to keep and the other drivers were driving safely, so we carried on.

I had made reservations at a hotel in a Chicago suburb, so we wouldn't have to go looking for a place while we were on the road. The only problem was that even though I had the address, I didn't really know where the place was. The map I had wasn't detailed enough. And greater Chicago is a very big place!

I know what you're thinking; why didn't I just turn on the GPS function on my phone and the nice lady will tell us where to go? But my phone was running low on power and I was afraid it would totally die and I wouldn't even be able to call and ask for directions.

We had a 12-volt receptacle installed just for charging my cell phone, but somehow in all the repairs, it didn't come to life. Or maybe it was the charger that wasn't functioning. In any case, we had a problem. So I solved the problem by getting the latest from the nice lady: "Go for ten miles on highway XX." Then I'd shut off the phone for those ten miles until it was time for the next installment.

Gerald gets a gold medal for his driving. He told me that Betsy had a lot of play in the steering even with the new steering box, so he had to keep his total focus on the road. If he let his gaze wander over to the gauges for even a few seconds, the car would start to wander off into the next lane.

Image little Betsy, chugging along at 40 miles an hour on wet pavement, getting splashed by every vehicle that passed us (and they all did), Gerald hanging on to the steering wheel for dear life, both of us soaking wet even in our rain jackets, with a windshield that made it seem like we were behind a waterfall. All of this made for the perfect storm.

At this point, I realized I had never been as miserable as I was right then. I didn't get a good night's sleep so I was tired. We were both wet from the leaking windshield and having to leave the windows open so it wouldn't fog up (but it did anyway). We were also cold, because the temperature was on its way to an overnight low in the 40s. I remember I started shivering somewhere in Indiana. And we hadn't had any lunch. So being tired, wet, cold and hungry is miserable. I remember praying on the Interstate; "Please, Lord, get us there safely." And He did.

We arrived safely at our hotel, heaved a sigh of relief, and realized how hungry we really were. The desk clerk referred us to Tony's Fresh Market – a really gigantic place where you could get lost if you weren't careful. We ordered some food from the deli counter and sat down at a small table for our supper.

We discovered that staying at hotels that provided a breakfast and stopping at a market with a deli was a fairly inexpensive way to get in two of our meals each day. It also saved time compared to doing sit-down meals at restaurants. At the markets, we could also stock up on munchies for lunch, like chocolate-covered nuts! Yummm.

Compared to Mom and Grandpa's first day on the road, ours was definitely more eventful, to say the least. I could have done with a little less adventure, but that is part of our title - An Ordinary Adventure.

CHICAGO IL TO LITCHFIELD IL 1934

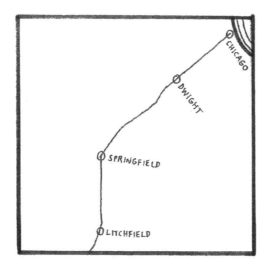

Instead of staying at a tourist cabin in Chicago, Mom had a local contact, Mr. and Mrs. Dekker. They were friends of Mom's boss, and showed Mom and Grandpa the best of hospitality. When they arrived, the Dekkers were just leaving for church, so they showed Mom and Grandpa their bedrooms, the dishes, the pantry and told them to help themselves.

In 1933, the World's Fair opened in Chicago. It was such a great hit that the city leaders and the organizers decided to reopen it for the next year. When Mom and Grandpa got there Oct 29, it was being dismantled for good, so some exhibits weren't open any more. But enough was left for them to get very tired walking around that first day.

Mom commented in her journal

Went to the World's Fair and arrived about 10 A.M. Walked continually - except during lunch – until 7 P.M. Took street cars both ways. Didn't even get lost although

we would have if we had followed Dad. Don't remember all we saw but it was very much worthwhile.

It was so worthwhile that they went back the next day, even though it was still very cold. They stayed from 10:30 am to 5 pm and were so worn out that they went to bed at 8:45 pm.

They were sorry to leave Chicago the next morning because they'd be leaving the "gas war" that was going on. The 8 gallons of gas they bought while in Chicago cost $1.11 – some of the cheapest gas of the whole trip!

Fortunately the rain stopped that Halloween morning. But Grandpa had a "slight accident" in Springfield, Illinois.

Nothing serious. Dad was driving and saw the car stop ahead, but just drove into it. We talked with the man and he and Dad settled the matter right there. Dad didn't learn to drive until he was 55, and never was a good driver.

Grandpa definitely had his driving troubles and this wasn't the last one. Perhaps because Mom learned to drive at such a young age, it was easier for her.

Their first stay in a tourist cabin in Litchfield set up a routine they would follow all the way to California. They would find a suitable tourist cabin – if there was one. Some they stayed in were barely habitable. Here's Mom's description of their first cabin:

Rented one with two beds, table, and chairs, running water, bedding and garage – all for $1.50. Dad retired at 7:30 P.M.

If you're not familiar with tourist cabins, they were the precursor to motels. Often times, they had cooking facilities (a hot plate), but no ice box. The mention of running water was a plus. I remember Mom telling of one cabin where they had to pump their own water from a well. Sometimes, there was no indoor plumbing, only an outhouse. Here's a picture of a 1930's era 4-unit tourist cabin that might have been like the ones they stayed in.

A 1930s Tourist Cabin

For some reason, Grandpa, who was a draftsman and pattern maker with the American Seating Company in Grand Rapids, would draw a floor plan of each cabin, indicating the furniture, bedding, and whether there was a heater and hot or cold water.

Here's his rendition of the tourist cabin in Litchfield:

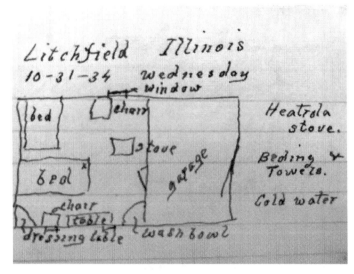

Grandpa's Floor Plan

46

This little drawing doesn't show the real expertise Grandpa demonstrated on the job after he educated himself. As was common in his era, Grandpa only had an 8th grade education. But he was determined to make something of himself when he realized that working at his job in a lumber camp wasn't going to be much of a future.

The only bright spot was the camp cook – a lively young lady named Ada (Adrianna) Vis. She was an immigrant from the Netherlands like Grandpa's forbears, so they could speak Dutch to each other when they didn't want others to understand too much.

As things progressed, Grandpa and Ada decided to make a future together – another reason to improve himself. So Grandpa took correspondence courses in algebra, geometry and drafting. His eventual employment with the American Seating Company in Grand Rapids provided a comfortable living over the years for Ada and their 7 children.

This picture shows the American Seating Company buildings today. It is quite a sprawling complex; much larger, I'm sure, than when Grandpa worked there from 1922 to 1945. If he were working there today, I'm sure he'd be amazed at the drafting tools available now.

The American Seating Company

His tools on this trip were the notebook and a pen.

While he was drawing his floor plan, Mom was cooking dinner:

Cooked our first meal since leaving home. I don't remember what our first meal consisted of, but we had brought potatoes, carrots and other vegetables with us, including rice. Each night when we stopped, after finding a cabin, we would go to a store and buy some sort of meat that could be cooked in a hurry, some milk and anything else that looked good, that could be eaten at that meal,

and bread for sandwiches for the next noon, milk, meat or cheese for the sandwiches.

After dinner, they went to bed. They were tired and there was nothing else to do anyway. The next morning, it was back on the road. Here's how it shaped up:

Most of the time, we did not stop for lunch. Dad would drive for a while in the morning and then I'd take over. While driving, Dad would hand me a sandwich, I'd take a bite and drink some water or milk out of a bottle that he'd hand me. We had bottles (usually a pint) each of water and milk. We'd use the milk for lunch and the water for the rest of the time. There was very little traffic on the road most of the time.

It was, after all, the Great Depression and travel for pleasure was not an option for a lot of people, but many were traveling to find better opportunities; this is the story of the United States since its founding.

CHICAGO IL TO LITCHFIELD IL 2017

Wednesday, October 25 dawned somewhat overcast, but no rain! This was really our first "official" day on Route 66 since it starts in Chicago. That means our rain-soaked day from Grandville to Chicago was merely an introduction.

We realized our first day out of the starting gate that we wouldn't have time to stop for lunch each day, so we did what Mom and Grandpa did – ate on the fly. We stayed at hotels that served a breakfast and would take some of their apples and bananas with us. We had already bought a big bag of mixed nuts and we had cheese sticks and water and teas. I ate while Gerald was driving, but he couldn't afford to take his eyes off the road or his hands off the wheel, so usually he didn't eat anything unless we stopped.

We were just getting used to not being tired, wet, cold and hungry when we rolled into the small town of Dwight. Route 66 took us directly through the town and we stopped at an old

Texaco gas station. It's no longer in business, but it's a very well-known tourist spot on the highway. In fact, Mom and Grandpa must have driven by or might have even bought gas here.

We were greeted by Maureen and Scott Sand, volunteers who were able to tell us about the station; that it was the longest-operating station on Route 66, from 1933 to 1999 – exactly 66 years! As the sign says, "Flats were fixed, breakdowns towed, and at times, the spirits of weary travelers restored."

Maureen and Scott

Maureen asked if we'd like to come inside the station and put a pin in the map to show where we were from. It turns out, there wasn't room! The map was just stuffed full of pins in Southern California. The same was true for Grand Rapids, so that didn't work either.

As I looked around, I realized there were maps of every continent. I saw pins in New Zealand, Australia, South America, Europe and – lo and behold! – I noticed a pin in Siberia! What would a person from Siberia be doing in Dwight, Illinois? Maureen said she was there the day that man came in. He was another Route 66 fan and had come all that way to drive the Route. I was amazed.

We also met another traveler who had driven his own car all the way from Alberta, Canada, to drive Route 66. He said he hoped he'd see us later on the trip, but I doubted he'd be that slow. Betsy's top steady speed is just about 50 miles an hour.

We said good-by to Maureen and Scott and continued on. As we were driving along on a fairly modern stretch which was labeled Route 66, we noticed some very old pavement alongside us. It was the original road!

It wasn't meant to be driven on, because we noticed every quarter-mile or so there would be a pile of dirt or a barrier. But there were access roads that crossed the old pavement, so we were able to drive up on one section for a photo shoot. Doesn't Betsy look right at home?

Betsy on Old Route 66

This is the actual road that Mom and Grandpa would have driven on 83 years ago.

Even though we had only gotten as far as central Illinois, I remarked to Gerald that it felt really good to be back in the Midwest. I said, "People are friendly, they are kind, they are thoughtful, they are helpful." He mentioned that San Diego was like that when he was growing up there. On this trip, we were going to have that experience of Midwestern kindness many times, starting with Jim Nichols (even if he is in California) and Paul Schultz and John Battjes in Grand Rapids being prime examples. But there were other times too. For instance...

The Ariston Cafe

When we got to Litchfield, we stopped for dinner at the Ariston Café, a Route 66 landmark. Back at the hotel, I realized I didn't have my black scarf. It wasn't in our room or the car, so I presumed I'd left it in the café. I asked Lisa at the front desk for help. Instead of just giving me the phone number for the Ariston, she called over there for me to ask if someone would look for my scarf.

A short time later, she called our room and said my scarf had been found. It had slipped onto the floor under the table and being black, I didn't notice. I figured we'd hop in the car and go get it, but she said someone from the café would drop it off. About 20 minutes later, she rang our room again and the scarf had been delivered – by the owner herself. What a kind gesture!

This made me reflect on the same sort of kindness and caring I have experienced in my church community. I had already noticed, and would continue to notice, the great number of churches in every city and town we passed through. I speculated that even if fewer people attend those churches today, they have been influenced by the teachings of Jesus; love God and love your neighbor as yourself, perhaps passed down from their grandparents and parents, aunts and uncles. It just seemed a part of the Midwestern culture.

Our experience so far had me musing about coming back to re-do our trip, only taking a lot more time. Not only would it be delightful to meet more friendly folks, but we could spend more time exploring all the things in our guidebook. This is a fantastic trip, but we're on a schedule, so each day we're hustling off to the next town. It took us eight hours to go the 245 miles from Chicago to Litchfield, which left us little time for anything else but driving.

LITCHFIELD IL TO SPRINGFIELD MO 1934

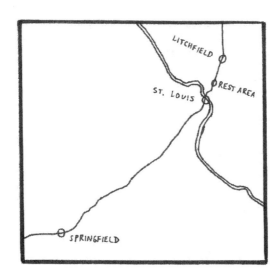

Mom's journal didn't indicate why they decided to leave Grandville late in October. Perhaps they figured they would miss snow in the Midwest and blistering heat in the Southwest. In any case, cold often accompanied them.

Leaving Litchfield at 9:30 am on November 1, they were greeted with

Weather – sunshiny but cold. Not very pretty traveling through Southern Illinois. Crossed the Mississippi River at St Louis at 11 am.

Since Litchfield and St Louis are 56 miles apart, this 90-minute trip meant they were zipping along at 37 miles an hour. Not bad for Route 66 in a Model A. After leaving St Louis, the landscape became more interesting as they started into the Ozarks.

From Cuba to Lebanon – about 90 miles – we went over the Ozark Mountains. Practically all we saw was hills,

valleys, and trees. The Ozark Mountains were very beautiful. From Lebanon on, we saw more farms.

They arrived uneventfully in Springfield, Missouri, and found a tourist cabin, with Mom remarking that is was "quite cold" during the night. Not surprising, since it was November 1.

In her meticulous way, Mom had recorded all their expenses so far. Here's what 5 days on the road totaled: $19.63. Lest you wonder why things seem so inexpensive, remember – it was the Depression and wages were in line with expenses.

For example, here's what happened to weekly wages during the first 3 years of the Great Depression:

NATIONAL BUREAU OF ECONOMIC RESEARCH, INC.

TABLE 1
AVERAGE PER-CAPITA WEEKLY EARNINGS, 1929 AND 1932ᵃ

Industry	1929	1932	Percentage change, 1929 to 1932
Manufacturing	$27.36	$18.18	—33.6
Bituminous Coal	25.00	13.78	—44.9
Anthracite Coal	30.85	24.86	—19.6
Metalliferous Mining	30.12	18.63	—38.2
Public Utilities	29.56	28.58	— 3.3
Trade, Retail and Wholesale	25.10	21.95	—12.6
Class I Railroads	32.62	27.15	—16.8

ᵃIt should be repeated that the samples from which these earnings are derived are of unequal value, so that much greater reliance can be placed on the figures for railroads and manufactures than, for example, on those for retail and wholesale trade.

Depression Wages Drop

That $19.63 was a week's wages for some workers – if they were lucky enough to still have a job. According to data from the Bureau of Labor Statistics, the unemployment rate hit its peak of 25% in 1933, just a year before our adventurers hit the road. And that doesn't reflect those who were employed but didn't earn enough to totally support their families.

Meanwhile, back with our trekkers, their most expensive day was October 31, when they settled up with the Dekkers in Chicago and bought provisions for the road trip coming up. You can see why Mom made such a good bookkeeper; she was meticulous, even to recording the two cent tax on their supplies. You'll also notice a record of the accident settlement in Springfield - all of $2.00.

Expenses so far

LITCHFIELD IL TO SPRINGFIELD MO 2017

Today would be one of our longest – 271 miles. At 40 miles per hour, that takes all day, including some stops. I wondered how long it took Mom and Grandpa. Mom didn't record their arrival time, so we have no way to compare our two days on the road. Our roads were better because we had to get on Interstate highways which now cover a lot of what used to be Route 66, but by comparison, in 1934 there was certainly less traffic.

Our usual custom after spending a few hours on the road was to stop at gas stations and rest stops. One stop east of St Louis turned out to be very interesting. We were finding that Betsy attracted attention whenever we stopped and it didn't matter where we were.

In this case, our rest stop was an official highway rest stop with flush toilets and all those wonderful modern conveniences. One man who approached us, David Longron by name, said he was a writer and was working on a book about Route 66. Not a tourist guide, but a book about what Route 66 means to people and what attracts them to it. We exchanged cards so we could look for each other's books on Amazon.

Other people came up to look the car over and when we found out they were locals, we asked them about the best route through or around St Louis. We were trying to stick to Route 66 as best we could, but when I read the directions for how to get through St Louis, I realized we might easily get lost more than once.

A Rest Stop Near St Louis

I was using Jerry McClanahan's *EZ 66 Guide for Travelers*, which has practically become the bible for Route 66 aficionados. His directions are meticulous and you can't go wrong if you follow them. But here's the excerpt that really scared me off:

*"**ST LOUIS**, gateway to the west, nests in a tangled web of roads and freeways. Over the decades, US 66 used a bewildering variety of streets thru the region: main, city, truck, bypass and optional routes made worse by later road building and One-Way streets."*

I had already found that going through cities was a very tense operation. Gerald had to keep his eyes on the road and I had to keep my eyes on the gauges, the guide book and the street signs. That's three responsibilities for only two eyes. Besides that, Betsy doesn't turn on a dime and if I missed a sign, we could easily overshoot a turn and then have to figure out how to get back on track.

I was sure Mom and Grandpa didn't have this problem, so I had no guilt at all about abandoning Route 66 until we got on the other side. Our local guys told us the best freeways to follow, and we made it safely around St Louis. Whew!

When it was time for another rest, the map showed a Route 66 State Park just over he Missouri state line and I figured that would be a good place to stop. It turned out to be a memorable event. When we pulled into the parking lot, we

Two Riders from India

were in interesting company – 2 BMW motorcycles. You may wonder what's so unusual about that. Well, they were from India!

The two men riding them were making a trip around the world. (Yes, they did ship them over the oceans.) They were with an organization called One World, One Ride and they were riding to connect people all over the world. One man was all set up with a small camera and a microphone on his leathers and helmet so he was able to film every conversation he had each day. Then some of those conversations would be posted on YouTube every day. What amazing things modern technology can do! If you'd like to find out more or watch some of their trip, go to www.oneworldoneride.in.

It made me think of the contrast between us and them making our separate journeys on Route 66 in relative prosperity compared to Mom and Grandpa making their trek in the midst of a world-wide Depression. Mom and Grandpa were fortunate that they both had jobs and could afford to leave them for a time to make their trip. For us, it meant Gerald just taking two weeks of vacation time, which was no big deal. Obviously, the fellows from India were also well-off, since they were taking much more time to go around the world. Musing about this helped us count our blessings.

We developed a great way to count our blessings each day. My dear friend, Margaret, who also gave us the Route 66 shield for Betsy, had given us a religious medal for our safety and protection. At first, I carried it in my purse. Then Gerald thought we should hang it

Our Companion Medal

from the rear view mirror, and it became our constant companion for the rest of the journey.

We soon developed an on-the-road ritual to count our blessings and thank God for the ones we had already received: Gerald would give our little "Jesus and saints" medal a gentle "thank you" squeeze each day as we got under way. Then he would pat Betsy's tiny dash rail, thanking her for running well, pat my leg, acknowledging, I presume, that without my navigation, we would be lost most of the time. Then I, in turn, would pat his leg, acknowledging that without his steady driving, we wouldn't get anywhere at all. The four of us made a great team!

After our ritual, we'd get started on that day's journey which usually included some Interstate highways. We'd often get some toot-toots from the semis that were whooshing by us. Gerald would respond with an "aoougah" from Betsy's horn, even though I don't think they could hear us. The motorcyclists would also give us a wave or a thumbs-up. One man was even taking pictures and videos from the passenger seat of a car as it passed us.

Something I enjoyed about our ride through Missouri were the highway signs to encourage safe driving. Here's one of my favorites: *"Avoid the monster mash. Buckle up."* We did buckle up with our after-market lap belts and fortunately never had to put them to the test.

We were approaching Springfield, Missouri, and it had been a long day. Considering the time of year, the sun was going down and we were headed straight for it. It was blinding Gerald and wasn't safe to continue. So we pulled off the highway and waited for about ten

Betsy at the Rail Haven

minutes until the sun went down over the horizon. Since it wasn't safe for us to drive in the dark, we only had a short time to get to our hotel before the fading light was gone. Fortunately, we made it.

Our abode when we arrived in Springfield was a favorite on Route 66 since 1938, when it was called the Rail Haven Motel. Even though Mom and Grandpa wouldn't have stayed here, we couldn't resist the charm of an authentic Route 66 relic. There were even re-created Burma Shave signs on the property, just like in the good old days:

> *This will never*
> *come to pass*
> *A back seat*
> *driver*
> *out of gas*
> *Burma Shave*

Those of you who are of a certain age will remember the Burma Shave signs with fond affection. Unfortunately, they went by the wayside after 1963 due to highway beautification and better roads which allowed faster speeds, but less time for reading the signs.

Another claim to fame for Springfield was the "birth" of Route 66 in 1926. There is quite a story behind the selection of that particular number. An organization called the American Association of State Highway Officials had been formed to select and designate a number of roads and highways that would form a

Springfield - The Birthplace of Route 66

national highway system, which up to the 1920s had been fairly random and disconnected between the various states. The leader of the association was Cyrus Avery, a resident of Tulsa, Oklahoma.

In the 20's there were over 250 marked roads and trails in various states and local boosters wanted their particular road included in this national highway system. There were known routes like the Santa Fe Trail that traversed the middle of the country and the old Butterfield Stage Line that ran fairly close to our southern border. But Avery wanted this new designated highway to pass through Tulsa for obvious reasons; he was a business owner there.

To avoid confusion, it was decided by the association to use numbers instead of names to designate these new highway routes. Odd numbers would be given to highways running north and south and even numbers for east and west. A shield would indicate a national highway and circular signs would be reserved for state highways. The important national highways would all end in zero and be less than 100, such as 40, 50 or 60.

Cyrus Avery and his cohorts from Missouri and Illinois decided the Chicago-Los Angeles route should be Route 60. But supporters of a highway from Virginia to Springfield, Missouri vehemently objected because that's the number they wanted. The matter was deadlocked. Avery had even ordered 600,000 Missouri state maps to be printed showing the highway as Route 60. Neither side would budge.

Finally, afraid of Congress stopping the whole project, Avery and his supporters resigned themselves to picking another number. At a gathering in Springfield, Missouri on April 30, 1926, they sent a telegram to the Bureau of Public Roads as follows:

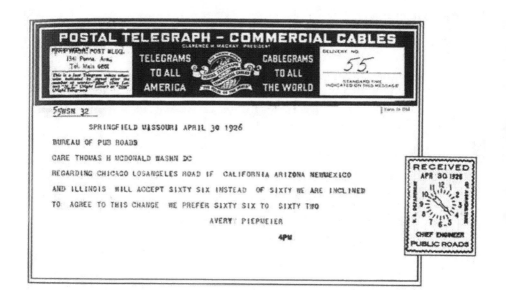

The Fateful Telegram

And that's the story of how Route 66 got its name. It does have a certain ring to it, doesn't it?

We didn't know all this when we arrived at the Rail Haven, but after over ten hours in transit which included our stops, we were really tired and turned in early.

Springfield MO to Tulsa OK 1934

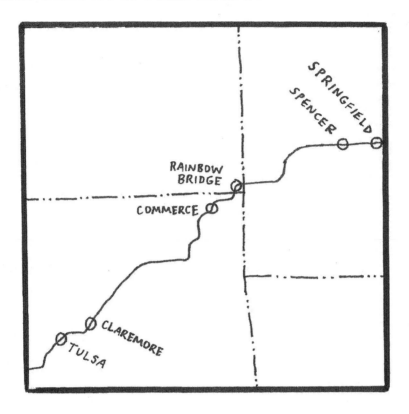

November 2 for our travelers was a day for driving through 3 states. Looking at the map shows how this was possible.

You'll notice Springfield, Missouri, on the right side and if you're really observant, you'll see that Route 66 goes through a tiny corner of Kansas before moving into Oklahoma. That little snippet of Kansas is short, but it counts!

Country quite level the remainder of the way through Missouri. Had another slight accident in Joplin, Mo. Drove about 13 miles through Kansas. Roads were not very good.

Those thirteen miles through Kansas weren't worthy of much comment back in 1934. But then again, Mom and Grandpa weren't sightseeing; they were trying to get to California as quickly as possible.

Roads were quite bad for about the first 50 miles in Oklahoma. We could not drive much faster than 25 miles per hour and sometimes not that fast. Very windy all day. Had a couple of detours too.

The route is over 180 miles, so you can see that going 25 miles an hour for part of the route requires over seven hours of driving, not counting any stops. Having driven this route ourselves, we know how tiring it can be.

The tourist cabin they rented was one of the finer ones, because it was worthy of its own entry for the day.

Tulsa is one of the prettiest towns we have been through so far. Found some very nice cabins near Tulsa. Rented one with two bedrooms, table, chairs, running water, toilet, shower, and gas plate and heater - $1.50. Rained a little in the evening. Retired about 8 bells.

People like us who retrace the old Route 66 don't have the experience of staying in the old tourist cabins. If running water, toilet, shower, gas plate and heater are worthy of comment, it makes one realize that these may not have been all that common. Grandpa once again fills us in on the layout:

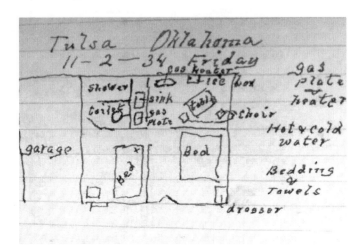

The Tulsa Floor Plan

Pretty classy, right? And all for $1.50! This one even had its own ice box. I remember visiting my Dad's mother in Grandville when I was just a kid in the early 50s, and her house had a wooden ice box. The inside was lined with metal as I recall and there was a compartment on the top just for the block of ice the ice man would bring. I don't know how long the ice would last, but I do remember it was a rule not to open the ice box unless you knew what you wanted, took it out, and closed the door really fast.

Icebox memories aside, even though this was a really nice cabin, the open road was calling again.

Springfield MO to Tulsa OK 2017

I began to see why Mom's journal entry for this day was so short; the countryside is pleasant, but there isn't much to see. As I was reflecting on what Mom and Grandpa had to do to complete this trip, I realized that we really couldn't retrace their exact trip. As I mentioned in Chapter 2, much of Route 66 just isn't there anymore. Either it has fallen into ruins and it's not drivable, or it has been covered up by modern highways and Interstates.

But such is life. Things will always change and the neighborhood we grew up in will never be the same as we remember. But there are other compensations, like meeting the two men from India who were motorcycling around the world. We can never recreate Mom and Grandpa's experience either because that is very individual. But we were creating our own experience.

Another realization hit us fairly early in our journey - we can't do it all. Because we were trying to follow Mom and Grandpa's itinerary, there was much we read about in Jerry McClanahan's guide book that we just had to pass by. As I mentioned before, that gave us the perfect excuse to plan more trips to visit what we didn't have the time to see now.

The Bridge at Johnson Creek

My reflection time came to an end when we encountered a photo op - an old 1926 bridge over Johnson Creek on our way to the remains of Spencer, consisting mainly of a defunct gas station and garage. Everything was very well-kept and tidy. Someone had done a nice job of restoration and I almost expected an attendant to come out of the station and offer to pump gas.

Since there was no one around, I had Gerald pose under the hood as if he were making repairs. But we could tell this was a gas station frozen in time – regular gas was only 12.4 cents a gallon!

The Gas Station at Spencer

Route 66 - East and West

Just so you realize how peaceful and quiet things were, here is the view from Spencer – looking east and looking west. Exciting, isn't it? But it does give you a look at an authentic stretch of Route 66, in this case paved with concrete. Not all sections were so modern.

As we meandered into Kansas, we were delighted to learn that none of Route 66 here has been destroyed, pushed aside or paved over by an Interstate highway, or as Jerry McClanahan calls it, the "superslab."

Even though Kansas hosts only 13 miles of Route 66, it's an interesting 13 miles. One of the first historic sights worthy of a little detour is the Rainbow Bridge. It is the last of the so-called Marsh Arch bridges, named for the designer. It almost seems like a

The Last Marsh Arch Bridge

work of art in its own right. What a shame that two of them have been demolished.

As a side note, we passed through the town of Commerce, Oklahoma. Its claim to fame is that it's the boyhood home of Mickey Mantle. You can still see his childhood home and a statue of him at the Commerce High School athletic field, also named after him.

A few miles further on, we passed through Claremore, the birthplace of Will Rogers, which seems to be a much bigger deal. Many places in town are named after him, and at one time it was proposed that Route 66 be officially named The Will Rogers Highway.

As we continued our travels, we came upon a section of old road that really caught my attention. From reading the sign and our guidebook, we learned that this is definitely a section of Route 66 that Mom and Grandpa would have driven on! It extends from Miami to Afton for a little over 15 miles.

A little internet research led me to a site that had all the records about the paving of what would become Route 66. This portion is exactly 15.469 miles long. It was graded, drained and then paved with a concrete base and curbs and then covered with a rock asphalt surface. The work was completed by the Western Paving Co. in 1922, even before Route 66 was officially

The Historic Ribbon Road 1922-1937

commissioned in 1926. It is still in use by the locals (and us tourists) today.

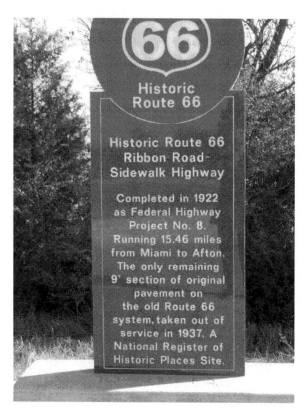

After this fantastic find, there was another one that had me scratching my head. We stopped at a gas station. No big deal, but I must mention that some of these gas stations are like small cities. They sell not only gas and snacks, but clothing, toys, tools, auto supplies and booze!

I went inside for a pit stop and as I was leaving, I noticed a barrel of ice by the door, full of bottles of beer! Now I figured the only reason for selling cold beer is because someone wants to drink it right away. Is that someone going to get behind the wheel?

Gerald got behind the wheel (without beer) for our last stretch to Tulsa, home of Cyrus Avery of Route 66 fame.

Tulsa OK to Elk City OK 1934

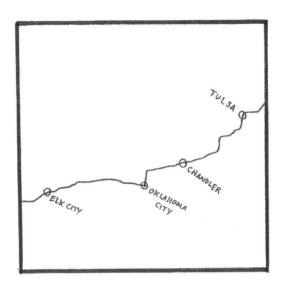

Mom mentioned it was cool and cloudy leaving Tulsa. Mileage – 50802. It was a day of noticing small things.

Very strong wind. Roads very good. Most all houses are small one-story affairs. Most of them are very pretty.

Ground, dirt roads, rivers, lakes, streams, etc. are all very red. Oklahoma requires just one license plate on each car – in the rear. Roads go under all railroad crossings.

When they got to Elk City, they found a true innovation in parking:

Parking problems are managed very efficiently in Elk City. Cars are parked in the middle of all streets. Angle parking at each curb is also practiced. The result is that you have to go about 10 miles per hour in order to keep from hitting some other car.

They found a nice cabin and settled into the daily routine. Even though red dirt and parking innovations may not seem too exciting, what happened the next morning almost ended the whole trip. Let Mom tell the story in her own words.

Dad's hair caught fire when he lit the gas heater. I became very dizzy while washing dishes and immediately threw up all my breakfast, then had to lie down, which put us behind about an hour.

Many years later, Mom recalled this incident in her commentary.

Our cabin was very nice, but the gas heater had a part broken out and when Dad leaned over it to light it, his hair and eyebrows caught fire. He ran his hands real fast over them and put the fire out. Dad was all ready to turn around and head back to Grandville, but I talked him out of that.

After traveling 1131 miles over that first week, it would have been a shame to abruptly end this Ordinary Adventure. Fortunately, they decided to soldier on through Texas, where they found a very different scene.

TULSA OK TO ELK CITY OK 2017

We thought we'd get an early start out of Tulsa, but found we had a problem. Gerald had put some of the special 20W-50 oil that Betsy needed into a big plastic jug that he kept in the front tool box that sat in front of the radiator. But the jiggling and jarring of driving on some of the old roads had worn a hole in the bottom of the jug and most of the oil leaked out. It turns out there was a bolt under the jug that was the culprit.

That had to be cleaned up before we could go anywhere. After using up a few rags and some old newspapers, we ended up in the local auto parts store for some new oil. The time was now 10:30 am. With sunset at 6:47 pm, we knew our limits. But we figured eight hours was enough time since we wouldn't be stopping for lunch.

We usually didn't stop for much else either, but today we'd be passing through Chandler, Oklahoma, the home of Jerry

McClanahan, author of our *EZ 66 Guide For Travelers*. He's a very friendly fellow, as is obvious because he put his address and phone number in the book. A quick phone call got us an invitation to stop by.

Jerry has his studio/gallery next to his home. We found out not only is he the expert on Route 66, but is an accomplished artist. He said he'd paint a picture of Betsy whenever we were ready.

Jerry McClanahan

Chandler is just east of Oklahoma City and when we successfully maneuvered through that big city, we were introduced to the wide open spaces of Oklahoma by the speed limits on I-40. The maximum speed was 75. No problem there. On her best day, Betsy could never dream of going that fast. But there was a minimum speed of 50. Not a problem for a modern car, but Betsy would need a slight downhill and a tail wind to go faster than 50 and keep it up. Since most of I-40 was flat here, we were able to maintain about 48-50 miles per hour. Considering Betsy was a dowager lady, no one tried to push her from behind or got impatient.

Since we had some long stretches on I-40, you might think Gerald and I would have some opportunity for long, meaningful conversations, but you would be mistaken. Our communication consisted mostly of yelling to each other over the engine noise, and then only when there was something important to say, like me reading the gauges to him or letting him know there was a turn coming up.

Later, we found an old stretch of Route 66 that paralleled the freeway, so we decided to take the authentic road. We found out along the way that Route 66 was either dirt, gravel, asphalt, macadam (crushed rock) or concrete. This stretch was concrete, so you might think it would be the best. Not so. When the road was paved it was done with slabs of concrete. Every time we drove over one of the seams between the slabs, we would bump, bump, bump, bump. Everything rattled, including us. So after about six or seven miles, Gerald said we had to get off the road to avoid damaging Betsy and head back to the Interstate.

Driving on the Interstate gave me more time to watch the scenery and ruminate. We saw our first oil well and lots of the red dirt that Mom had mentioned in her notebook. In addition to that, another common thing I noticed again was the great number of churches in every town, just as I had mentioned in Chapter 7 on the way to Litchfield. It was the same in Missouri and now Oklahoma. Just as before, the people we met were friendly, helpful, polite and kind. Whenever I went up to the counter in one of the gas stations to pay for my lunch provisions, the sales clerk would say, "May I help you, ma'am?" I don't think I've ever been addressed as "ma'am" in California.

Likewise, I noticed that when Gerald was approaching the door to the gas station, some younger man would open the door for him and say, "Let me help you, sir." My previous speculation in Litchfield about the reason for this was confirmed many times on this trip. It was very noticeable and much-appreciated. There's a lot to be said for the culture of the heartland of America.

Our final destination, Elk City, was very welcome. We checked into our hotel and asked about a good place for dinner. "The Cowboy Café" was the answer. We headed on over and when we walked in the door, a lady asked, "Are you here for the Bible study?" We thought that an odd question when entering a restaurant on a Saturday evening, but the lady explained that the owner was a former pastor and thought a Bible study in his restaurant would be a great thing. It would have been interesting to stay, since I'm a Bible teacher of long standing, but that wouldn't take the place of dinner, so we moved on to the Chinese restaurant across the street.

This was our fifth day on the road. We were both very grateful that Betsy was performing as well as she had been, considering all she had been through. Gerald had been an absolutely fabulous driver. I had total confidence in his ability. But I know we were both very tired at the end of the day. How could I tell? We were both under the covers before 9 pm. Now I understood why Mom and Grandpa went to bed so early.

ELK CITY OK TO TUCUMCARI NM 1934

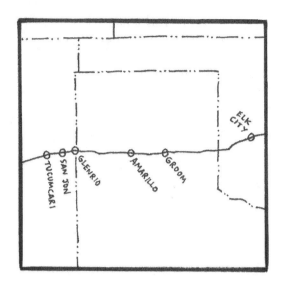

Having been to Texas a few times and driven through it once many years ago, I found that Texans are, by and large, very proud to be Texans. Texas was, after all, an independent country for ten years before becoming a part of the United States and don't you forget it!

Unfortunately, Mom didn't find this part of Texas terribly interesting. In her own words,

There are no large signboards on the highways in Texas. There are also no trees. Nothing to look at but miles of waste land, a few cattle and horses – some of them in the road – and once in a while a farmhouse.

We ran into a sandstorm which obstructed our view beyond a one-half mile radius and also obstructed the sun's rays, but beyond that was not very serious. All gravel roads were extremely dusty. Rear left tire went flat in New Mexico near San Jon – on pavement and we found no nail in it.

They might have been happy to get out of Texas, but to have another flat right over the state line was the pits. The nail in the tire would have to be fixed, regardless of the cause. If it had happened to us, we would just call AAA on my cell phone and Gerald would coach the driver on how to fix flats in tube tires. But not in 1934.

Mom didn't say she helped Grandpa, even though she KNEW how to fix a flat. (Remember in Chapter 3 where her brothers MADE her learn how to change a tire?) Grandpa got out the jack, the tire irons, the patch kit and the tire pump and jacked up the car. Fixing the tire wasn't just a matter of putting on the spare. That only works the first time you have a flat. After that, you have to fix it the old-fashioned way – by hand. And they had already used the spare on their first flat.

Grandpa first had to jack up the car, then take the wheel off the axle. Next, he had to carefully use the tire irons to pry the tire off the wheel. That would expose the tube, which he could then extract from the tire to inspect for leaks.

Next he would look and feel inside the tire for nails or anything that could have caused the leak. In this case, he found nothing. Then he inspected the tube to find the leak. Partially inflating the tube might reveal the leak right away. If not, he'd have to use the water test; put water on the tube and see if you've got any bubbles coming out of it. If you don't have any water handy, use spit.

When he had located the leak, he dried and abraded the leaking spot, put on some glue, removed the backing from the patch and carefully applied the patch over the leak and the glue, making sure he had good adhesion.

So far, so good. But now he had to do it all in reverse. He had to carefully put the partially-inflated tube back in the tire, making sure there were no wrinkles. Then he had to carefully replace the tire back on the wheel, making sure he didn't damage the tube with the tire irons. And don't forget, the valve on the tube had to be lined up with the hole in the wheel.

When that was all done, the next job was pumping up the tube so the tire had adequate tire pressure. Now that he had a fully-inflated tire on the wheel, he had to put the wheel back on the axle. When he was finally finished, Grandpa deserved a rest!

Flat tires weren't the only adventure on the road. With little scenery to look at and not much to do on this stretch of eastern New Mexico, Mom decided for some reason to look at her driver's license –

It had EXPIRED! Then dad decided to check his, and his had also expired. So we drove the rest of the way across country with expired driver's licenses.

Saw Tucumcari Mt. 30 miles before we got to it. Set watches back another hour – to Mountain Standard Time. Retired at 8 P.M.

They finally arrived at their destination, Tucumcari. I'm sure they wondered where the town got its funny name. And I bet you're wondering too.

Back in the late 1700s, a Comanche burial record mentions a battle at Cuchuncari, which may have lent its name to Tucumcari Mountain and eventually the town. As is the case with so many Western towns, Tucumcari started its life as a railroad construction camp. The evolution of names is a hoot; Ragtown became Six Shooter Siding (due to the numerous gunfights) and finally Tucumcari in 1908.

ELK CITY OK TO TUCUMCARI NM 2017

We had a few adventures leaving Elk City that made our time there more memorable. Previously, Gerald had noticed that one section of water hose to the engine was bulging. Duct tape to the rescue! I quickly went inside the station where we were getting gas to buy some duct tape. (I mentioned before that these stations carry everything.)

The man on the other side of the gas pump noticed Gerald's head under Betsy's hood. He was a highway worker and his vehicle had all sorts of repair goodies. When he found out the problem, he gave us some strapping tape to hold the duct tape in place. Another sign of Midwestern kindness.

Before we left Elk City, Gerald also wanted to replace the turn signal flasher which hadn't been working for a day or so. We found another auto supply place and got a new one. When he took out the old one, it was full of water. Where did the water come from? Our first rainy day on the way to Chicago!

Now that we felt Betsy was ready for the road, it was time for breakfast, so we decided to try the Cowboy Café again. We met Shannon, who was delightful and filled us in on the Saturday Bible study we had stumbled into the night before. Having a Bible study at a place that people frequent (like a restaurant) seems like a good idea. She said the owner would like to expand the idea to other places. I asked her where else people hang out in town. She said, "the bars." Well, if a Bible study in a restaurant works, why not a Bible study in a bar? She didn't think Elk City was quite ready for that yet!

We couldn't leave town without a stop at the National Route 66 Museum. Every state on Route 66 has its own museums, but this one, being a national one, was over the top. It was a re-creation of a 1930s small town with shops, tractors, outbuildings, windmills and a barn.

National Route 66 Museum

Unfortunately, being a Sunday, it was closed.

Now we were entering that long stretch of the Texas panhandle that Mom had written about; ***Nothing to look at but miles of waste land, a few cattle and horses – some of them in the road – and once in a while a farmhouse.*** According to the Texas State Historical Association, even the Spanish explorer Coronado was of the same opinion. In a letter to the King of

Spain on October 20, 1541 he wrote: "I reached some plains so vast, that I did not find their limit anywhere I went, although I travelled over them for more than 300 leagues . . . with no more land marks than if we had been swallowed up by the sea . . . there was not a stone, nor bit of rising ground, nor a tree, nor a shrub, nor anything to go by." I also had to agree there wasn't much to look at except the roadkill.

As I recall, I saw armadillos, a dog, a badger, a deer and many raccoons, possums and skunks that had met their end on the highway. But what I found strange was that all of them were neatly laid out on the shoulder perpendicular to the flow of traffic. I have no explanation for this. Maybe there's a roadkill undertaker.

In one area, we again decided to drive on the authentic Route 66 pavement. We had quite a view; Route 66 just a few feet from I-40. The terrain was so flat, there was no doubt which way the road went. Don't swerve the wrong way either, or you could find yourself aiming at a giant semi. We were riding on concrete slabs again, so we had the bumpy ride, but not as bad as Oklahoma.

Route 66 and I 40

The Largest Cross

Having such a featureless landscape may be what prompts people to build things on a massive scale. For instance, did you know the Western Hemisphere's largest cross is in Texas? It is located near the town of Groom and it's as tall as a nineteen-story building. You can stop and take a tour and also view the Stations of the Cross.

However, the all-time winner for Texas "big" is the Big Texan east of Amarillo. Many people have heard of this place where, if you eat a 72-oz steak with all the trimmings in one hour, it's free. So we had to stop. We didn't stop to eat, but we did talk to one fellow who had actually done it. He said he didn't want to do it again, however.

Bigger Than Betsy!

At our next stop for gas, Betsy was really the center of attention. A car had pulled off the road because of her. A man named Julian and his wife Brianna, along with her sister, just happened to be driving by and decided to learn more about this beautiful Model A. We must have chatted for at least 20 minutes. During that time, the station owner came out and we all had a nice story-telling time.

Of course, we had to tell about Betsy and about Mom and Grandpa making the Route 66 trip in 1934 in a Model A. We pulled out the pictures we carried in the door pocket and the time flew by.

Julian asked if he could take a picture of the car. Of course! Nearly every place we stopped, people would ask if they could take pictures. Betsy was a full-fledged celebrity! It was obvious that this trip would not be the same if we didn't have Betsy. People just loved her, they loved the story and they all wished us well. These stops certainly made the trip more memorable for us.

Back on the road, we noticed LOTS of big semis. Not too surprising, since I-40 is the major east-west route in this part of the country. Next time you go into a store or order anything online, remember that the things you buy were probably transported by truck in order to get to your doorstep.

West of Amarillo we saw cows, cotton and windmills - the power-generating kind hundreds of feet tall. I wondered how long the farmers here could continue to grow their cotton. All crops require water and this wasn't an area that got a lot of rainfall. That means groundwater has been pumped out for irrigation. But researchers tell us the huge Ogallala aquifer, which is the principal source of water for most of the farms and ranches, is being depleted at an increasing rate and may be fully depleted by 2028. This would create dire consequences eventually, but we didn't learn what plans might be afoot to mitigate this possibility.

When we came to the border with New Mexico, we took a little side trip to the now-defunct town of Glenrio. Formerly, it was a small, but bustling Route 66 town, but being bypassed by I-40 in 1973 was its death knell, as is true of so

A Relic of Glenrio

many other once-thriving towns. But it lives on in the movie version of *Grapes of Wrath* because some of the movie was filmed in Glenrio. It was sad to see how little was left. I wondered what had happened to the people who used to live there.

Our eventual destination was Tucumcari, New Mexico. And the only place to stay in Tucumcari for die-hard Route 66 fans is the Blue Swallow Motel. It was recommended to us by someone we met in Missouri! It was one of those don't-miss places,

The Blue Swallow

restored to look like it did in 1939. Too bad Mom and Grandpa missed it.

Our Blue Swallow Garage

We discovered there were enclosed garages next to each room, and we saw in one of those garages a 1929 Ford Model A pick-up truck. It belonged to the owners, who were very interested in comparing notes with us.

They also recommended a great place for dinner – the Pow Wow Restaurant. Since we'd been sitting in the car for so long each day, we welcomed the opportunity to walk to dinner. But this was not your ordinary restaurant.

We were amazed to find that each booth had portraits of locals painted on the wall and they appeared to be eating with us. Note the woman and her two granddaughters. Don't they look realistic?

The Pow Wow Restaurant

Our other find was a talking lizard. I didn't know it talked until our waitress invited us to have our picture taken with said lizard. I must have jumped a foot when it greeted us! I'm sure this was fun for the locals to watch the gullible tourists get sucked into posing with a talking lizard.

This was one of our longest days – 279 miles. So we went back to the Blue Swallow and crashed. Well, Gerald crashed. But every evening before I crashed, I would record my notes for

The Talking Lizard

the day with a description of every picture I took. This particular day, I took 28 pictures. If I had not done that, I'm sure I'd have a lot of pictures that wouldn't be very useful because I wouldn't remember where or why I took them.

One thing I found very interesting was that Mom and Grandpa evidently didn't take a camera with them because I've never seen any pictures of this trip. I'm quite sure they had something like a Kodak Brownie because I've seen other family pictures taken around the same time back in Grandville. Maybe they figured they wouldn't have time or it was just one more thing to carry. So we had only Mom's little notebook and her commentary to go by.

TUCUMCARI NM TO ALBUQUERQUE NM (2 DAYS) 1934

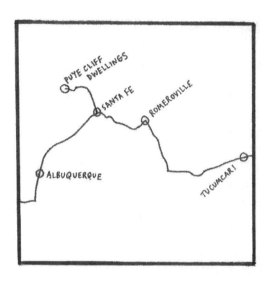

A cool sunny day greeted our travelers as they left Tucumcari that Monday. But this day was not going to be remembered as one of their favorites. Here's why:

Very bad roads from Tucumcari to Romeroville – a distance of about 120 miles. The car bounced all over the road at the top speed of 20 to 25 miles per hour. Two dishes broke due to the jarring.

Had pavement 67 miles from Romeroville to Santa Fe. Also had another flat tire today – on the pavement.

The scenery was very beautiful. We rode miles and miles without seeing houses. Rode between mountains the biggest share of the day.

Climbed all inclines on high but went down one incline so steep we had to put the car in second gear. Averaged about 24 miles per hour all day. Arrived at Santa Fe at 4 P.M. The streets are quite narrow. Weather became quite warm and we drove with the windows down and our coats off.

I'm sure they were happy to have finally arrived. Even though the cabin they found was the nicest so far, Grandpa's lack of driving skill became evident once again.

Dad backed the car into one of the porch pillars of the cabin and broke it. I killed flies in the cabin for about one hour. Dad washed all the dishes before we could cook supper because they were just loaded with dust.

The city of Santa Fe, founded by Spanish colonists in 1610, is known as the oldest state capital in the United States and the oldest city in New Mexico. The city's original full name was and still is *La Villa Real de la Santa Fe de San Francisco de Asís* ("The Royal City of the Holy Faith of Saint Francis of Assisi").

Being such an old and historic city, Grandpa and Mom decided to explore a few of the local sights. One of those was the Old San Miguel Chapel – the oldest surviving church in the continental U.S. and noted as such in Mom's notes. They also visited the Rockefeller Laboratory of Anthropology, the Historical Society Museum and the Palace of the Governors. Originally constructed in the early 17th century as Spain's seat of government for what is today the American Southwest, the Palace of the Governors chronicles the history of Santa Fe as well as New Mexico and the region. This adobe structure is the oldest continuously occupied public building in the U.S. and is now the state's history museum.

The Palace of the Governors was located north of Santa Fe – perhaps ¼ or ½ mile. There were lots of old maps which showed the US without any west coast.

These must have been very old maps Mom was writing about, since Juan Cabrillo explored the west coast of what is now the United States and died during his expedition in 1543. It's believed he's buried on one of the Channel Islands west of Santa Barbara, California. After his death, the Spanish claimed the land and began recording their voyages.

Meanwhile, their sightseeing was going to continue north of Santa Fe, but that never happened. Here's why:

We got the car all greased, etc. and left Santa Fe at noon to go to Frijoles Cavern and also to Puye to see the Cliff Dwellings. We rode 15 miles north of Santa Fe on the pavement and then turned off onto the worst corduroy road in the U.S.A. We progressed at the fine speed of 10 miles per hour and after going 14 miles (there were 16 more to go) including a 4½ mile climb up the side of a mountain, we decided to go back rather than to go on and wreck the car on that road, and our dispositions too.

Thus they finally arrived in Albuquerque. Finding a very nice cabin in Albuquerque brightened their spirits somewhat – two rooms and bath, gas plate and heater and plenty of chairs. For the first time they used their own bedding.

They were now 1707 miles into their Ordinary Adventure.

TUCUMCARI NM TO ALBUQUERQUE NM (1 DAY) 2017

We had such a good time at the Pow Wow Restaurant the night before we were happy to go back for breakfast. Things were kind of slow that Monday morning so our waitress had time to fill us in on the local situation. She said it was unfortunate that a number of people are living on welfare and seem to prefer that to working, even when jobs are available, because reality sets in when they find working takes up time and taxes take part of their paycheck. She also mentioned drugs are a problem, especially for the young people. We had found that to be an issue in other parts of the country where we have traveled.

We realized that many of the smaller towns and cities are struggling economically. The young people who may leave to get an education often don't come back to live. The smaller family farms and ranches have been consolidated by agribusiness into vast tracts, and industries have moved out to larger population centers or overseas or for various other reasons. Sometimes tourist dollars aren't enough to keep the economy pumped up, even on such iconic Route 66 cities as Tucumcari.

After breakfast, we got back on the road where I saw the longest railroad train I think I've ever seen. Having little else to look at, I counted cars. There were two engines, then 60 cars, then three engines, then 49 cars, and lastly, one engine. There were cars as far as the eye could see. These were all box cars and they were headed west. The next train I saw was three engines and 94 cars. Each car was loaded with two containers.

Other trains we saw were loaded with coal. I speculated they were headed for the coal-fired electric plants in the Four Corners area. Later I discovered there are coal-fired electric plants outside Winslow, Arizona, much closer than the Four Corners area I was thinking about.

A Train over the Horizon

I've discovered that many times when I've ordered things online and I get them the next day, they have come from a warehouse in Las Vegas, a city on I-15. Both the semis on the Interstate freeways and the railroads we were seeing have made this kind of commerce possible.

Compare that with the state of transportation in 1934. Yes, there were rail lines and highways that went cross-country. The Lincoln Highway was one of the first to link the east and west coasts under one name in the early 1920's. And of course the golden spike was driven in Promontory Point, Utah in 1869, uniting the country by rail. But that didn't mean driving or taking a train cross country back then was easy or comfortable.

We also found out driving the same kind of car as Mom and Grandpa on modern roads was not without its own challenges. Fortunately, Gerald has been a "car guy" since the age of 15 or so, and it paid off. He felt Betsy was running rough and thought there might be an issue with the transmission. So we stopped at a gas station to check.

In order to access the transmission box to check the oil level, he had to remove the rug on the floor of the passenger side, pry up a cover and use a dip stick to check the level. He found it was dangerously low. Since there is no gauge for this kind of thing, he was going by his instinct, which was correct in this case.

He had the foresight to take along extra bottles of this extra-thick transmission oil and after a few glug-glugs, it was back up to the proper level. Had he not sensed something was amiss, we could have ended up in a very bad situation with a non-functioning transmission.

Now that Betsy was back in fine form, we headed for Santa Fe. I recalled a previous family vacation Gerald, Brendan and I had taken there in 1997 – exactly 20 years earlier. Before we left for that trip, Mom told us when we got there to go to the Palace of the Governors and we would see the

The Palace of the Governors

Navajo Indians under the portico selling their silver jewelry. She was 87 at the time and remembered that scene as clear as a bell.

When we got there, it was just as she described. I remember standing in front of the Palace with tears in my eyes, thinking that I may have been standing in her footsteps, but 63 years later. It was a memorable moment. Now, 20 years after that scene, I was again standing in the very same place and it looked just as it did in 1997. Thanks for the memories, Mom!

Another place not to be missed in Santa Fe is the Loretto Chapel, built in 1873. Even though we had visited it on our previous trip, it was definitely worth a second visit. As the story goes, after New Mexico became part of the United States in 1848, the Bishop of Santa Fe, Bishop Lamy, put out an appeal to the Sisters of Loretto to come and teach the children of Santa Fe. They responded and opened their first academy in 1853.

The Loretto Chapel

The sisters wanted to have a chapel to complement the academy and finally were able to raise the funds. After five years of construction, the chapel was dedicated in 1878. They were able to secure the services of the same French architects who were also designing and building the St Francis Cathedral downtown. The Loretto Chapel is an architectural gem with beautiful stained glass, statuary and reredos, the display of Jesus and the saints behind the altar.

However, by far the most unusual architectural feature is the famous staircase. Often chapels in Europe were built without a staircase to the choir loft because it would take up too much seating space. Ladders were used instead, which worked out fine because only the men would be using them. But this chapel was for the sisters. What to do? The sisters decided to pray about their dilemma to St Joseph, the patron saint of carpenters and the earthly father of Jesus. On the ninth day of prayer, an old man who said he was a carpenter came to the academy and offered to build the staircase.

The sisters hired him on the spot. The staircase took six to eight months to complete and was finished without banisters or railings, nails, screws, glue or a center support. The only thing holding everything together, even today, is hundreds of wooden pegs. The underside was finished with horsehair plaster.

The Miracle Staircase

The sisters would crawl up the stairs by putting one hand on the stair ahead of them, the other one holding their habits out of the way. Coming down was often accomplished by crawling down backwards or bumping down on their bottoms. It must have been quite a sight. Some years later, railings and balusters were added for safety. After it was finished, so the story goes, the carpenter disappeared without a trace and without being paid. A miracle?

The Oldest House

Since Mom and Grandpa had to go right by the Loretto Chapel to go from the San Miguel Church to get to the Palace of the Governors, they couldn't have missed it, but Mom doesn't say whether they went inside. After our visit to the Palace of the Governors and the Loretto Chapel, we headed to the Oldest House, where Mom and Grandpa had stopped. It's hard to say if this is the oldest house still standing in the U.S. but tree-ring specimens, taken from some of the vigas (beams) in the ceilings of the lower rooms show cutting dates of 1740-67. Part of the building has kept the form of a house, although it's no longer used as such. The remainder of the building is a curio shop.

The Oldest Church

Not too far away is the San Miguel Church. Coming from California, we're used to missions, since we have 21 of them, founded by Fr. (now Saint) Junipero Serra and other Franciscans. This church looked very much like a mission church you would see in California. It is claimed that the San Miguel Church is located in a place that has been a sacred site for the Analco natives for over 800 years. The current building dates from 1610 – ten years before the Pilgrims landed at Plymouth Rock.

Much of our history is focused on the eastern portion of our country, starting with the Pilgrims and the Puritans and later revolving around the British colonies and Virginia. We often think of the history of our country progressing from east to west. But the Spaniards had come from Mexico and settled in Santa Fe in 1607, which created a movement from south to north. And then we can't forget the Russian influence in Alaska and Northern California, dating from as early as the 1740s until Alaska was purchased by the U.S. in 1867.

It's interesting to explore this part of our heritage. If not for certain events of history, our common language might be Spanish or even Russian instead of English. My ancestors came to this country speaking Dutch and Gerald's with a heritage of Irish Gaelic. We are certainly a polyglot nation of many languages.

Being a history buff, I really wanted to explore more of Santa Fe and try out my rusty Spanish, but once again the open road was calling. We reluctantly left, resolving to return at a later date to savor more of the flavor of this historic old city.

ALBUQUERQUE NM TO HOLBROOK AZ 1934

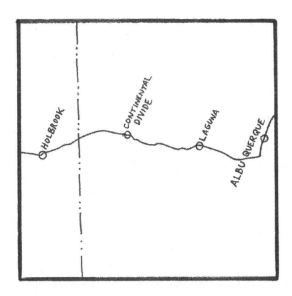

Even though it was November 7th, the weather was warm and sunshiny...So warm riding today that my face and left arm are sunburned.

Saw two flocks – about 100 each – of sheep being driven down the main highway of Albuquerque. (I'm sure that *doesn't happen anymore!) Had good roads most of the way. Had two short detours. Came over several cattle guards and dips. These are just places where the road is built into a stream, in place of a bridge. Practically all streams and rivers are dry. Saw sand dunes way up in the mountains at Laguna, N.M.*

Something that was new to them was Indians – lots of Indians:

Some walking, some riding horses, or in wagons or autos, some making pottery, beads, etc. and selling same. Saw several Indian Pueblos today. Most of the houses have large strings of funny looking red things hanging up to dry. Also corn and hides.

When we were in front of the Palace of the Governors, we also saw long strings of "red things" hanging. Mom didn't know they were chili peppers, since they aren't grown in Michigan.

They found a suitable cabin in Holbrook and for the second time, had to use their own bedding.

ALBUQUERQUE NM TO HOLBROOK AZ 2017

Albuquerque certainly has an unusual name. I learned it was named in honor of Francisco Fernández de la Cueva, 10th Duke of Alburquerque who was Viceroy of New Spain from 1702 to 1711. If you're sharp, you've noticed the difference in spelling; the Duke's name has an extra "R". This is because the original name belongs to a city in Spain, near the Portuguese border. Supposedly the name derives from either Latin or Arabic and refers to oaks that grow in that area from which cork is produced.

While we were there, Gerald thought Betsy needed an oil and filter change, so he asked me to look up the nearest oil change place. A Jiffy Lube was only two miles away, so first thing in the morning, I called and found out they could take us right away. The charge would be $43.99. I told the man we had our own oil and filter, suitable for Betsy.

Well, when we got there the scenario changed. The men working there were all excited about working on a Model A, so Gerald hung out near the work area and answered questions. When one of the men asked where we were from, he told him Los Alamitos, California. As it turns out, that man graduated from Los Alamitos High School! And another one was from Bellflower, about 5 miles from our home. What are the chances?

Since we supplied our own oil and filter, the manager only charged us $36, but Gerald gave the guys a $20 tip, since they had also lubed everything and looked over the undercarriage. Once again, Betsy worked her charms on everyone who met her.

I did wonder later about what Grandpa did for oil and filter changes. I don't imagine there were too many service stations outside of the towns. It was only mentioned a few times in the notebook about when they needed to service the car and that was always when they were in a town. These days, the gas stations on the Interstate are like small cities in themselves.

The Open Road

We left Albuquerque and headed into the wide open spaces on old Route 66. There is just the road and not much else, but we saw beautiful mesas of red rock. The contrast in color between the red rock and the sparse greenery was quite noticeable. The area around Albuquerque is pretty much desert, which accounts for the lack of vegetation. The average rainfall for November is just over .5 inches.

The red rock we saw is actually volcanic because two tectonic plates are pulling away from each other; the Colorado Plateau on the west and the Great Plains on the east. Filling this gap is the Rio Grande River. Of course, all this took eons, but the evidence is still visible.

We were headed for the Continental Divide, which wasn't at too high an elevation here. On a previous trip in Colorado, when we crossed the Continental Divide at over 10,000 feet, I was really out of breath.

Here we found out we were at "only" 7245 feet. But I noticed I was still huffing and puffing a little. But that meant it was all downhill from here, right? Wrong. We still had to drop to the elevation of the Colorado River and then climb back up to go over Mountain Pass in California which is over 4000 feet. But that all lay ahead of us.

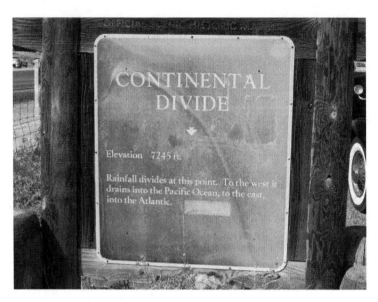

The Continental Divide - 7245 ft

We saw more long trains of 60 to 100 cars with containers double stacked, transporting goods thousands of miles. Compare that to 1934 when most people ate food they had grown or which came from local farms. Some goods were transported long distances, but nothing like what we were witnessing.

Cars like Betsy would have come from one of the 35 Ford assembly plants in the U.S. But not everyone had cars in 1934. According to the U.S. Department of Transportation, in 1900 there were approximately 8000 cars registered in the entire United States. By 1934, there were 21,472,078. And this was for a population of 126,037,000. So there was one car for every six people. Compare that to today, where many families have two or more cars. Obviously, car production and ownership is one of the great industrial success stories in our history.

We continued our trek across New Mexico and went through Gallup, but didn't need to stop. Just after we crossed into Arizona, I heard a strange noise coming from the front of the car. In this picture taken earlier, you'll notice the authentic desert water bag hanging from the front bumper. It was

Betsy and the Water Bag

really there for show. It did have water in it, but we never used it for the radiator. We discovered the noise I heard was the bag self-destructing. The rope holding it on was never designed for the speeds we had been driving on the highways and Interstates. The bag was pretty well shredded, so we had to remove it – a victim of technological progress. So much for authenticity.

By this time, we were quite close to our destination – Holbrook AZ. When in Holbrook, you definitely have to stay at the Wigwam Motel. Like the Blue Swallow Motel in Tucumcari, the Wigwam Motel wasn't there when Mom and Grandpa went through Holbrook, but who can pass up the chance to stay in an authentic (sort of) wigwam? Actually, we learned later they were more correctly called tipis.

Stayed in a Wigwam Lately?

Originally, there were six Wigwam Motels around the country, built between 1933 and 1949 by Frank Redford. They started in Kentucky (#1 & 2) and expanded to Louisiana (#3), Florida (#4), Alabama (#5) and California (#6). The one in Holbrook (#7) was built in 1950 by Chester Lewis, an admirer of the original developer. Only three remain; #2 (probably because it's close to Mammoth Cave National

Our Wigwam

Park), #6 in Rialto, California and #7 where we stayed. What makes the Holbrook one so interesting is the lobby, which has many interesting artifacts with a small museum in the back displaying some early pioneer and Indian artifacts.

The manager suggested Romo's for dinner and it was a fine place to eat. Shades of Elk City, three men came in, took a table near us and it was obvious they were doing a Bible study over dinner. It was a short lesson, though, because this was the final night of the World Series. When we got back to the Wigwam, the TV was going in the lobby, so we joined the manager and her husband to watch the game. She was very happy when Houston won because she didn't like the Dodgers. I wasn't as concerned about who won the game, but I thought after Hurricane Harvey devastated Houston, the people there might like something to cheer about.

The World Series was already over by the time Mom and Grandpa started on their trip. But if they had wanted to keep track on the road, think of it: no radios or TV in their rooms, no Wi-Fi, no cell phones or tablets to get the latest scores. The best they could do would be newspapers. If they bought one, they would have found out the St. Louis Cardinals beat out the

Detroit Tigers, winning in seven games for their third championship in eight years.

After the game, part of our conversation turned to the local economy. As in so many other towns we had passed through, Holbrook would be in dire straits if the Arizona Power Service followed through on its plan to close down the Cholla coal-fired power plant, where many of the locals work. It's a four-unit plant and unit two had already been shut down in 2016. The issue is environmental. To upgrade the plant to meet emission standards will cost millions and that cost will be passed on to consumers. There is talk of converting it to natural gas or even solar, but those options are also costly. It made me think that these are some of the same issues people faced in the Depression; loss of local jobs on a massive scale. Then what?

It was getting to be bedtime, but my body and my brain were confused. Arizona is one of the states that does not observe Daylight Saving Time, Hawaii being the other one. Both states contend they get enough daylight and heat year round and moving the clock twice a year is unnecessary. So when we crossed the border from New Mexico into Arizona, we should have still been on Mountain Daylight Time. But Arizona was on Mountain Standard Time, which was the same time it was in California, which was on Pacific Daylight Time. Got that? Me neither. So I just flopped into bed, figuring my body would know what to do.

Mom and Grandpa didn't have to deal with this unless they were in an area which had a local law establishing some form of daylight saving. It was tried during World War I and II to make more daylight hours available and conserve fuel for the war efforts. But it was a hodge-podge in various states and even counties and cities until Congress passed the Uniform Time Act of 1966, which is basically what we have today. States may opt out by passing a state law, which is what Arizona and Hawaii have done.

Regardless of what time zone we were in, we still tried to get a good night's sleep for the next day's drive, not knowing what conditions we'd have to face.

HOLBROOK AZ TO WILLIAMS AZ 1934

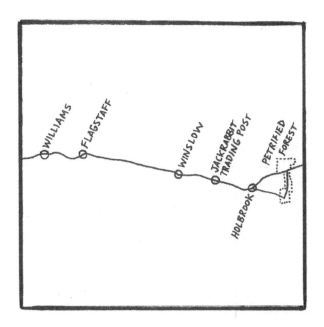

Our intrepid travelers continued their adventure the next day by visiting the Petrified Forest, which was only 19 miles away. They had never seen anything like this in Michigan!

Their first stop was the Museum where they saw

Indian handicraft, specimens of petrified wood, fossil leaves, fossil head of an animal resembling a salamander, and also the head of an animal related to the dinosaur family. Walked through Rainbow Forest which contains the largest tree trunk which is 5 feet thick thru the trunk and 7 feet through the base.

Then walked through the Third Forest which contains many long trunks which are all intact, the longest being 125 feet.

We also saw what is called the agate house. It has been reconstructed on the original foundation and still has the original stone implements inside with a crude ladder going up through the roof. The house was supposed to have been used 900 years ago.

Walking through the Second Forest, we saw many segments of petrified wood that were all light in color and looked so very much like wood that we had to feel of them to convince ourselves that they were really stone.

We saw the most noted petrified log which spans a cavern and is called Agate Bridge. We walked a little farther and had to sight along two nails in a small signboard to see Pedestal Log which is way across a valley and is a log about 8 feet in diameter which forms a pedestal because of erosion.

It was time to get back to Holbrook because their ultimate destination was Williams. Just after they left Holbrook, they had a strange encounter:

We were stopped by an officer who asked where we were going, etc. and put a little green O.K. sticker on the windshield.

Mom didn't explain why they were stopped and evidently needed a sticker. Maybe it was because they were from out of state.

One thing that caught Mom's attention in both New Mexico and Arizona was what they saw alongside the roads. You can tell that this was very different than what they were used to back in Michigan:

We noticed that fence posts were just overgrown sticks, that on one side of the road is a track to be used by horse-driven vehicles, that the roads were paved with oil and not cement such as we have, and that some large streams or small rivers are called washes.

As they continued on shortly after leaving Holbrook, they were greeted with a new sight:

Saw a mountain in the West when we were 4 miles west of Joseph City and drove 72 miles before we got to it. It is about 5 miles east of Flagstaff, is called San Francisco Peak, is 12,794 feet high, the highest spot in Arizona.

Anyone who has ever driven in the area knows that the mountain range called the San Francisco Peaks dominates the local landscape. But for accuracy, we must correct Mom's notes. The highest peak is Mt. Humphries and it's only 12,633 (or 12,637) feet in elevation. Not to be too picky, but why is the elevation given differently in two different sources? And why are both of these different than what Mom had in her notes? And why did she note that the high mountain they saw (Mt Humphries) was east of Flagstaff instead of north? I don't know.

Thus was their introduction to Flagstaff and Williams, where they decided to stay for the night.

HOLBROOK AZ TO WILLIAMS AZ 2017

The Cholla Coal-Fired Plant

While we were at the Wigwam Motel, we asked the manager about a good place for breakfast, since they didn't provide it there. She said we should go to La Posada. When I asked her where it was, she said it was in Winslow, which is just the next town down the road. So we set out for what we presumed was just a nice restaurant. We didn't figure we'd have time to visit the Petrified Forest as Mom and Grandpa had done, but we had been there on a previous trip.

On the way, we saw the Cholla Power Plant we had talked about the night before. This may be where the coal in those long trains was going. Closing it altogether would mean a huge loss to the local economy and up to 500 jobs would disappear. When we returned from our trip, I did some research and found out that indeed, there is a schedule for closing the plant. The closure is scheduled to begin in 2023 and be completed by 2028. Anyone could easily see the power plant driving by and not even realize the economic hardship that may fall on this area in a few years.

One of the iconic places everyone looks for on Route 66 is the Jackrabbit Trading Post. Back in the 1940s and 1950s, they had put their signs along Route 66 for miles in either direction to attract the travelers. Each sign would have the Jackrabbit logo and the number of miles until you got there. The anticipation would build until you saw the giant billboard: "Here It Is!" By that time you had to stop. But since we had to make more miles that day, we decided not to stop.

You're Almost There!

Entrance to La Posada

In a very short time, we arrived in Winslow. Driving through, we sensed this was like so many other towns we had driven through – until we came to La Posada. We were expecting a restaurant, not an elegant hotel, restaurant, gift shop and historic edifice that had recently been saved from destruction. We knew Mom and Grandpa would never have stayed in such a fine facility, but this was going to be our breakfast stop. And there is quite a story to tell.

The Fred Harvey Company teamed up with the Atchison, Topeka and Santa Fe Railway to design and build all the hotels and restaurants at the various train stops across the country. The chief designer and architect for Fred Harvey from 1902 to 1948 was Mary Colter, a milestone for a woman in that day. She not only designed the buildings for La Posada, but the gardens, the furniture, the linens and the china. She won further accolades for the design of six of the most well-known buildings in Grand Canyon National Park.

After an investment of about $2,000,000 (equivalent to $40,000,000 today), La Posada opened on May 15, 1930. Every passenger train between Los Angeles and Chicago stopped there. In fact, the train station was right at the front entrance. Route 66 went by the back entrance. What could be more convenient? But the timing was terrible due to the Depression and then World War II, and La Posada never really hit its prime, even though it was a fabulous place. Finally in 1957, it was closed because plane travel had impacted La Posada too much. After I-40 was completed, even travel along Route 66 dwindled in that area.

In 1959, all of Mary Coulter's custom furniture was auctioned off or destroyed. Finding no buyers for the building, the Santa Fe Railway finally gutted the facility and made it into offices. The gardens were paved over for parking. By 1993, the railway decided to move its offices and tear down the buildings. But all was not lost! A local effort was begun to save the building. A hero in the person of Allan Affeldt heard what was going to happen to La Posada and decided he would join the effort to save it from destruction. So he started the fund-raising necessary to buy the place and he and artist Tina Mion moved in and proceeded to begin the restoration. This was 1997 and the work still continues today.

After we were waited on in the Turquoise Room by an "authentic" Harvey Girl in her signature black and white uniform and savored an absolutely fabulous breakfast, we took some extra time to wander around the building and visit the gift shop and bookstore. We decided this was definitely a place to return to.

Our Very Own Brush Fire

Back on the road, Route 66 has all but disappeared between Holbrook and Williams, a victim of the super-slab. It does make for faster traveling, however, even at our top speed of 50 miles an hour. About the most exciting thing we saw was a brush fire. Living in California, we are very familiar with these. We just managed to scoot through, because my trusty smart phone told us the highway department was closing the Interstate in the area we had just passed through. Fortunately, the rest of our trip to Williams was uneventful.

WILLIAMS TO THE GRAND CANYON AND BACK 1934

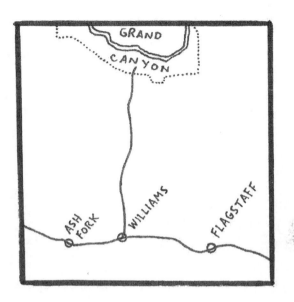

Mom and Grandpa took an extra day to visit the Grand Canyon. How could they not, after coming all this way?

It surely is a marvelous sight. Walked 1½ miles toward the east along the footpath to the Museum. Looked through about a dozen telescopes at the canyon. Walked back to the car, ate lunch, bought postcards and mailed some, and drove west along the edge of the Canyon and stopped at all the observation points.

Here was one of the most interesting:

Went out on one point which extends several hundred feet into the Canyon where a memorial is erected to a Mr. Powell who was the first man to go through the Canyon by boat.

Obviously they weren't familiar with Major John Wesley Powell, a one-armed Civil War veteran who led the now-famous Powell expedition from Green River Station, Wyoming through the Grand Canyon to the mouth of the Virgin River in Nevada. They left in May of 1869 and arrived about 100 days later.

The Powell trip wasn't a piece of cake, either. They had brought some food stores with them, but planned on hunting along the way. Little did they know that the canyons were almost devoid of game.

They lost one of their four boats – the one with most of the food stores. So they went as fast as they could and barely escaped starvation. Three of the men may have decided the expedition was doomed and left the party at what is now called Separation Rapids. They were never seen again. It's interesting to speculate whether these three men leaving the party allowed just enough food for the rest to survive. We will never know.

After visiting the Canyon, I'm sure Mom and Grandpa had much to talk about on the way back to Williams, where they again spent the night.

WILLIAMS TO THE GRAND CANYON AND BACK 2017

I believe the Grand Canyon is one of the very special places every American should visit. I have been there a few times and it is awesome every time I look into that great yawning chasm.

I recall the time I was with Gerald for his first visit. We parked at the first overlook we came to and I watched as he walked up to the edge of the overlook for his first view into the Canyon. His jaw literally dropped and he was speechless.

Many years ago, when I was much younger, I took the mule trip to the bottom of the Canyon. It sounds easy, since the mules were doing the hard work. But I got dehydrated and experienced mild heat prostration and was pretty well confined to my bed at Phantom Ranch and couldn't even wobble to the dining room for dinner.

Another time, I fared much better hiking down to Phantom Ranch. I guess I was in better shape and was drinking more water. It was very tiring, but I just put one foot in front of the other and made it down – and back up. And I survived.

My third adventure in the Grand Canyon was an eight-day trip on a pontoon boat down the Colorado River, launching at Lee's Ferry below Glen Canyon Dam and continuing to the take-out point at Temple Bar in Lake Mead. There was one important lesson that I still recall from that adventure; after being out of contact with "civilization" for those eight days, the news wasn't any different. It was still bad; only the names had changed.

All these thoughts were going through my mind as we wended our way up the highway to the Canyon.

I'm sure our trip north on Highway 64 was a lot different than Mom and Grandpa's. First and foremost, I'm sure the road is better maintained, since Grand Canyon today welcomes over four million visitors each year, up from 140,220 in 1934. There were two lanes in each direction until we got closer to the entrance station, when the two northbound lanes blossomed into five, and each was full to the brim. We were probably about 1/2 a mile back when the slowdown started, but we

Grand Canyon Entrance

had no problem gaining entrance with Gerald's Golden Age Passport – the best $25 we ever spent many decades ago.

Getting in was one thing; finding a parking place was another. There was nothing in Grand Canyon Village, or Lot 1 or 2 or 3 or 4. Fortunately, we found a spot near the Park Headquarters, complete with restroom. Our plan was to walk from there to the Rim Trail so we could see into the Canyon, but I became very weak and felt like I wasn't getting enough oxygen to carry on. I had forgotten that one doesn't acclimate to over 6800 feet of elevation quickly. So we headed back to the car for Plan B.

Since it was becoming more and more crowded anyway, we decided to head west along the road that leads to Hermit's Rest and the Powell Memorial which was a main attraction for us, since Mom had specifically mentioned it in her notebook. The road west has a number

The Grand Canyon

of overlooks so we could get a peek into the giant fissure in the earth that is the Canyon. Even after seeing it a number of times in years past, it has never ceased to amaze me with its sheer immensity.

We easily found our destination, parked the car and started walking down the path toward the Memorial. I had to clap my hand over my mouth to stifle a cry. Once again, I was struck by the same feeling I had at the Palace of the Governors in Santa Fe; my mother and grandfather stood here and walked this same trail. It's hard to describe this feeling of connection to my ancestors. It was almost as if they were there, albeit invisible to me. The connection felt stronger with my Mother since Grandpa passed on when I was only nine years old. Once again, a few tears welled up as we walked along.

This Way...

It's not just family that engenders this feeling of connection. Some years ago, we re-traced part of the Lewis and Clark Trail as closely as we could by car. In Montana, we came to a spot that Sacagawea, who was an invaluable guide to the expedition, recognized as a limestone intrusion called Beaverhead Rock. Our guide book told us to climb a low promontory and we could see Beaverhead Rock in the distance. It was this view that Meriwether Lewis wrote about in his journal.

As I stood in that spot, I looked down at my feet and realized that I must be standing right where he stood, since there weren't many other places to stand that were level. What an exciting experience for me, who used to teach American History to high-schoolers. It's experiences like this that make me a great believer in field trips for students and family trips with kids to explore what our great country has to offer; historically, geographically and culturally.

Standing near the Powell Memorial, I didn't realize how massive it was. I was expecting something much smaller, but then it struck me what a major accomplishment it was for Major Powell and his group to be the first recorded expedition to traverse the Canyon by boat. My Grand Canyon "expedition", by comparison, was vastly different, with experienced guides and boatmen and much more modern equipment.

The Powell Memorial

You might think that one hazardous trip through the Canyon would be enough for Major Powell, but not so. Because he and his companions didn't complete all the investigation they intended the first time, another expedition was launched in 1872 and completed successfully.

The Anniversary Medallion

After we visited more overlooks, we headed back to El Tovar Hotel, a place with some fond memories. When our son, Brendan, became engaged to Noelle, who is from Arizona, we went to meet her family one Thanksgiving in Mesa, near Phoenix. Later, the four of us drove into the park for dinner at El Tovar restaurant, which is really classy in a National Park sort of way – rustic but elegant. Noelle, in her eagerness to impress her future in-laws, managed to spill her wine on the nice white tablecloth. Despite that, once they tied the knot in 2005, it has remained firmly tied.

Because of the parking situation, Gerald dropped me off at El Tovar so I could get some pictures and he would circle around to pick me up. While he was circling, I decided to zip into the gift shop and found the perfect fridge magnet and coffee mug – all in about one minute. I found him outside and we decided it was time to head on back to Williams.

We approached the entrance/exit station and were dropping our jaws at the line-up of cars waiting to get in! We didn't clock it, but I'd estimate the line was at least three miles long. And it was 2:30 in the afternoon; it was going to be getting dark in a few hours! What were they thinking? We gave Betsy a pat on the dash and headed on down the road, glad we had come when we did.

WILLIAMS AZ TO SEARCHLIGHT NV 1934

Mom and Grandpa stopped in at a local garage to get the car fixed since it jerked. Then once again they were on their way.

Left Williams at 10 A.M. and drove to Kingman, where we turned off US 66 to take the road leading to Boulder City. Road was poor from Kingman for about 30 or 40 miles. Saw a sign instructing us to turn left to go to Boulder City. Took it. The road looked better than the road we were on and was better.

The new Boulder Dam (later to be named Hoover Dam) was under construction and they figured it would be quite a sight.

On the map above, you notice that to get to Boulder City, you must cross over the Colorado River. Today, they would be following US Route 93, a nice paved road that would take them directly to Boulder City. But back in 1934, conditions were very different. They headed north to a road that turns west, the Cottonwood Road, and headed for the Colorado River. To get there, they had to traverse the Black Mountains. Little did they know what an adventure this would be.

The road was a one-track affair and we very gradually went up into the mountains but came down much more abruptly. We came down the side of a ridge of mountains which was so steep we had to put the car in first gear the majority of the distance. We came down and down for 8 miles and then followed a very sandy road 3 miles to what is called the Aerial ferry.

And therein lies a tale. When they reached the river across from Cottonwood Cove they encountered the Cottonwood Aerial Ferry. And this is what it looked like:

The Aerial Ferry

You can find this picture in the archives of the University of Nevada, Las Vegas. Here's what was written on the photo sleeve:

"Cottonwood Aerial Ferry, from about 1930-1935. This was the last and the most unusual of several ferries that crossed at Cottonwood between Searchlight, Nev. and Chloride, Ariz., these being the two major towns in the area before 1920. Most were conventional barge types similar to the Arivada Ferry shown in another picture. The aerial

ferry was powered by an automobile engine mounted on the upper framework, with the operator up with the engine. It was located at the mouth of Painted Canyon, a short distance upriver from the Cottonwood Cove Resort. Courtesy Ella Kay."

Now imagine yourself arriving at the Aerial Ferry, noting the $2.00 fee to cross the river, and then actually driving your Model A onto that platform! There are only 8 cables supporting the entire contraption.

Many years later, when Mom was in her eighties, Gerald asked her how they got across the Colorado River since there were no bridges. She described their experience – undoubtedly the most unusual and harrowing of the entire trip. She told us that the car engine that ran the whole thing was out of a Model T. The operator would chock their tires and then climb up the ladder to crank over the engine and they would putt-putt slowly across the mighty Colorado. (Too bad you can't do this today. The remnants of the Cottonwood Aerial Ferry now lie under Lake Mojave, created by Davis Dam which was completed in 1951.)

I think Gerald had a hard time thinking of his 80-something mother-in-law telling the story of herself as a 24-year-old being gutsy enough to ride across the river on what he thought must have been a very flimsy contraption. I think he gained a new respect for her after hearing her fascinating story. We don't know whether it was Mom or Grandpa who actually drove the car onto the ferry, but it must have been a brave move, whoever did it.

Once they had completed the crossing, they followed another sandy road west for 15 miles up a gradual incline to Searchlight, Nevada. It was in Searchlight, a typical mountain settlement where

We rented the worst cabin we have had so far. It was the only cabin in town with two beds, and no doubt just as good as any other in town. The cabin is plenty large and looks like it was built by one of the forty-niners with no improvements since.

It has two rooms, the sides of which are wood and the ceilings covered with either duck or oil cloth painted several times but not in recent years. There are plenty of windows but no curtains and not enough shades to go around. Parts of the walls are covered with tin. All the furniture, we are sure, came over in the Mayflower.

The two beds are hollow in the middle and higher at one end than the other. The stoves are also relics. The tables are very crude affairs covered the same as the ceilings. The floor is covered with several old remnants of linoleum. The chairs are wired so that they won't fall apart.

An old commode serves as a wash stand with a pitcher and wash dish (with a rag in a hole in the bottom of it). Water supply was limited so we could have only two pitchers of water for washing ourselves, dishes, cooking, Dad's shaving, etc. One door stuck and we had to pry it open. There is no running water and no sink. A slop jar serves as the receptacle for dish water, etc.

There are two electric light bulbs, one in each room, which are supposed to light the place but being only 10-watts each, they didn't do much good. A kerosene lamp helped a little more. The electric lights were shut off promptly at 9:20 P.M. so we just had to go to bed.

The toilet accommodations were so dirty and old that we could hardly stand it – just the plain common mountain variety of two-holers.

We set our watches back another hour. We now have Pacific Standard Time.

It seems very obvious that Mom must have been holding her nose the whole time they stayed in that cabin. It couldn't have been much worse.

Mom didn't mention anything about Peach Springs in her notebook, but after leaving Williams, you can see from the map that Route 66 makes a turn towards the northwest to arrive at that outpost in the Hualapai Indian Reservation.

That was a good place to stop and replenish our snacks and make a pit stop, so we stopped at the gas station/store. As usual, Betsy attracted some attention in the parking lot, but of a most unusual kind. About five or six young people gathered around, but only one of them talked with us in heavily-accented English. They were a church group from France traveling with their chaperone! I don't know if they were Route 66 trekkers like us, but they were definitely interested in Betsy and our trip. We were getting used to meeting people on the road, but this was one of the most unusual. We never knew who we would meet next!

After leaving Peach Springs, we headed for Kingman where we had another interesting parking lot encounter. We met a couple from Birmingham, Alabama, who were making a cross-country trip on Harley-Davidson motorcycles. And I thought our trip was adventurous! These unexpected meetings certainly added interest to our trip, and maybe to the other folks' also.

Continuing on, we had to deviate from the route Mom and Grandpa took, because it's impossible to cross the Colorado River on the aerial ferry, as I mentioned previously. But we tried to find evidence of where it launched and landed.

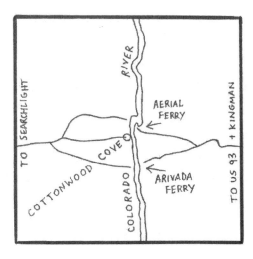

We tried approaching it from Searchlight on the west in order to find some evidence that the ferry was running back in the '30s. The map here and at the Cottonwood Cove Ranger

Station shows dirt roads converging on what was the Colorado River from the west and the east south of the current Cottonwood Cove.

According to the National Park Service, these roads led to and from the ferry landing for the Arivada, which provided ferry service across the river from 1916 to 1920, but was no longer in service by the 1930s.

But, according to the NPS, "There was also an aerial cableway built one mile north of the present Cottonwood Cove. It transported automobiles across the river on a rickety framework. It was said once you crossed the river to the other side, you would never come back. It was in operation until the 1930's."

In talking with Jane Overy, the founder and current director of the Searchlight Museum, she said she had spoken with some old-timers back in the 1980s who remembered crossing the river on the aerial ferry in the 1930s.

In the Searchlight Museum

We also found more evidence about the ferry in the Searchlight Museum. In the 1930s, the only way to get to Chloride, Arizona on the east side of the river from Searchlight in 45 miles was to go over the aerial ferry. It could be boarded at the river, only 14 miles east of Searchlight.

Even to this day, Gerald is still fascinated by the story of the aerial ferry. In fact, he keeps a picture of it in Betsy to show to people when we stop and talk.

SEARCHLIGHT NV TO MOUNTAIN PASS CA VIA BOULDER DAM 1934

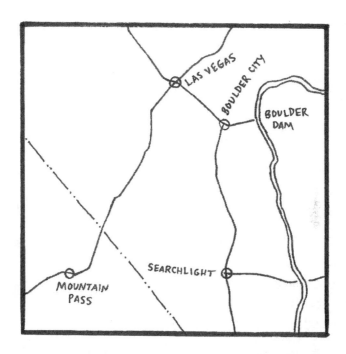

It was November 11, a warm and sunshiny Sunday. Mom and Grandpa left Searchlight about 9 am; mileage 52394. Mom's meticulous notes once again launch another day. And this would be an exciting day – they were going to see Boulder Dam!

Although they arrived at Boulder City at 10:45, they had to stand in line an hour to get a ticket to see the dam. And it wasn't until 1:45 before a guide could actually take them on the tour. But it must have been worthwhile, because Mom wrote a lot about their visit and what they learned.

Surely is a marvelous piece of work. Boulder Dam is about 8 miles from Boulder City and downhill all the way.

Saw the plant where the large pipes are made in sections 21 feet long and 30 feet in diameter. Drove way down in back of the Dam. The scenery was beautiful. Mountains of solid rock all around.

The dam is built 125 feet under the river bed. Boulder Dam will be 727 feet high and is 650 feet thick at the base. The crest of the Dam will be 1180 feet long and the width 45 feet, on which the highway from Kingman, Ariz. to Boulder City, Nevada, will cross Black Canyon. The reservoir back of the Dam when full will contain 30,500,000 acre feet of water and extend upstream 115 miles.

The installed capacity of the power house will be 1,835,000 horsepower. Several very large cables span the chasm from Nevada to Arizona on which are carried the huge pieces of pipe, which weigh 75 tons each.

The ends of the cables on the Arizona side go into the rock for 85 feet and are held solid by 50 feet of concrete. The other ends on the Nevada side go into the rock for 50 feet and have 35 feet of concrete.

Other cables carry huge buckets of concrete. These buckets when empty weigh 2 tons and when filled weigh 16 tons. Still other cables carry cages of 25 men each and lower them into or raise them out of the canyon.

Four tunnels were made to detour the Colorado River around the construction work. However, only one is being used at the present time.

The Dam is 18 months ahead of schedule. We saw motion pictures of operations at the Dam from the beginning of the work to the present time.

Boulder City is a very pretty little town, having been built in 18 months. The U.S. Government built the city, and expects that the rents collected will pay for the city by the time the Dam is completed. The houses rent for $5 per room per month.

Here's what the dam looked like in 1934

Boulder Dam Under Construction

When she was in her eighties, Mom told us that she and Grandpa had stood on what is now the bottom of Lake Mead. All the water from the Colorado River had been diverted through the four giant penstocks or "pipes" as she called them. The riverbed needed to be dry so the silt could be removed for the pouring of the concrete.

It seems amazing that the dam was 18 months ahead of schedule after 3 years and was eventually finished two years early. That was possible because the workers were busy on three shifts a day, seven days a week. There were no breaks for religious services or legal holidays. And there were plenty of men who applied for the dirty and dangerous jobs. Since so many were unemployed, it was a welcome source of income. Many brought their families with them. They originally lived in an encampment called Ragtown while they waited for Boulder City to be built.

Considering the amount of ink Mom expended describing this man-made marvel, I'm sure they were both very impressed. But after their tour, it was time to move on.

There were no cabins vacant at Boulder City, and at Las Vegas the same situation existed and we were instructed to go to the Chamber of Commerce and they would assign us rooms, but we didn't want to do that, so started toward Barstow and stopped everywhere we saw cabins for rent. Found one at last at an oil station up the in mountains. No town or city, but the station is named Mountain Pass and is in California.

Crossing into California was not the easiest thing to do in 1934. So many stricken farm families had left their land in the Dust Bowl of Oklahoma and nearby states (the Okies and Arkies as they came to be called), that California set up "bum barricades" at some parts of the California state line, mostly for those entering from Arizona.

Obviously, Grandpa and Mom were not "bums" so they would not have encountered the problems of some of the Okies and other Depression "refugees" as they tried to cross into California. Many were turned back with nowhere else to go.

BOULDER CITY AND BOULDER DAM 2017

The Dam Today

Boulder Dam is indeed an impressive sight, especially when you walk across the top of the dam and look down into the abyss. The word "huge" isn't quite adequate to describe the sight, but coming up with a superlative better than that is a challenge. The dam was officially named Hoover Dam in 1947 by an act of Congress, but I'm going to call it

Boulder Dam, because that's what Mom and Grandpa called it in 1934.

There is quite a history to the dam. The original concept predated the start of the Depression, it was finally dedicated in 1935 and the final touches finished in 1936, two years ahead of schedule. But why build a dam out in the middle of nowhere, in a canyon that seemed inaccessible? The answer – floods and power. The Imperial Valley in southeastern California was fertile farm land, the rich soil being a product of eons of previous floods that left a thick layer of silt. But the Colorado flooded repeatedly between 1902 through 1907, leaving behind not only devastated farm fields but also a souvenir – the Salton Sea, a product not only of flooding, but also a poorly-designed irrigation canal. The farmers were looking to the Federal government to prevent any more destruction of their fields and their livelihood. There were also growing demands for power from the cities of Los Angeles and Phoenix.

Finally in 1920, the Reclamation Service, under the direction of Arthur Powell Davis (Davis Dam was named after him) started planning for a massive water project - a dam, a canal, power generation and irrigation. The sale of the electricity generated by the dam would be used to pay for the dam itself. Congress authorized the Boulder Canyon Project in 1928 and construction began in early 1931. Here's the BEFORE picture:

Black Canyon Dam Site

123

There was much discussion and investigation about where to build the dam. Boulder Canyon was the first proposed site, but it was later found to have a fault line running through it. So the builders finally settled on Black Canyon, about eight miles downstream. Now consider this; we have the Boulder Canyon Dam that was actually built in Black Canyon and later renamed Hoover Dam. Whatever you call it, it is massive and Mom's statistics from her notebook are very accurate.

Overlooking the Dam

We had visited Boulder Dam many years before and it hadn't changed any except for the new parking structure carved out of the hillside on the Nevada side of the dam. We were very fortunate we found a parking spot so we could do the walk over the dam and take some pictures. In the background, you can see some of the giant electrical towers that carry power to portions of Nevada, Arizona and California.

The next time you flip a light switch in any of those areas, you might be tapping into that giant power grid.

Seeing this as a finished project, I can't imagine what two travelers from small-town Michigan must have thought about it. They had recently come from the Grand Canyon, itself a massive sight, but which had been carved over millions of years, ironically by the same river that was now being dammed to control its seasonal fury. And it would take only five years to do it.

Before we left, I wanted to find a book about the building of the dam. Being used to National Park visitor centers, which usually have lots of books, maps, and various souvenirs, I was surprised to find almost none of that at the dam site. Ah, but this was not a National Park! It was administered by the Bureau of Reclamation. I did manage to find one book that told about the history of the dam construction from a technical point of view.

We drove out of the parking area with one last glance at one of the largest man-made structures on earth.

Boulder Dam from the upper road

MOUNTAIN PASS CA TO RIALTO CA & UNCLE JOE'S HOUSE 1934

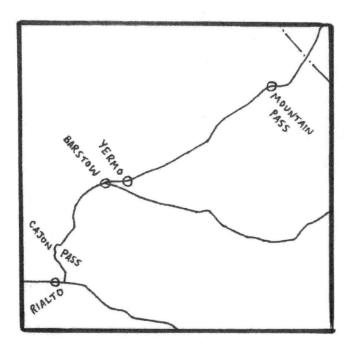

As Mom wrote in her notebook, Mountain Pass was an *oil station. No town or city.* Even today, Mountain Pass is not a real town, just a few buildings serving the rare earth mine that is nearby.

The next day was going to be the culmination of a looong, rough road and not a few hardships. But there is a digression that must be told before they get to their destination – Uncle Joe's house in Rialto, near San Bernardino.

Here's how Mom remembered the story many years later:

My mother always paid cash for everything. She and Dad went to look for the Model A when they decided to get one,

so Mother went back the next day with the money, and when the man asked for the name (to put on the title), she just said "Mrs. Isaac Van Koevering".

Since Mother didn't drive, I always got the license plates. I would write her name and sign mine underneath as "agent", but after she died, I went to get them and thought I should tell the lady that Mother was deceased, and she wanted to know if her estate had been probated and when I said it had not she said that she could not sell me the plates.

I wondered how we would get the plates. Then I thought I would do as I always had, so I went to the bureau (to another woman who apparently had not seen me before), and got the plates.

Mom was certainly not a dishonest person, but <u>not</u> telling the second agent about her mother's death did the trick!

This became what could have been a sticky issue when our weary travelers entered California. Many states back then required a permit to enter that state in a car with license plates from another state. So their Michigan plates meant they had to stop at a "port of entry" and get one of these permits, which would be good until December 31, 1934.

This permit station was in Yermo, which is near Barstow on the way to Rialto and Uncle Joe's house. So Grandpa pulled over just a little past the building and went into the station to get the permit while Mom stayed in the car.

When the agent was checking the registration, he saw the car was registered to "Mrs. Isaac Van Koevering" – now deceased. But the agent didn't know that.

While Dad was in the little building, the man there looked out the window at the car, saw the back of my head, and I believe he deduced that I was "Mrs. Isaac" so gave Dad the necessary papers.

So we went on with expired driver's licenses and in a car that didn't apparently, belong to either one of us!

After that adventure, I'd like to say it was a straight shot to Uncle Joe's house, but they had to traverse Cajon Pass. Their poor car had certainly gotten a workout, going from the aerial ferry at river level to Boulder Dam at about 500 feet above sea level, over Mountain Pass at 4728 feet, down to Yermo at 1929 feet and back over Cajon Pass at 3776 feet.

They also had a little car trouble.

The car died on us at Hicks and we found the condenser had broken loose. Dad wired it on and we had no more trouble.

Then Mom ends her notebook with these uneventful words:

Arrived at Uncle Joe's house in Rialto, California, at 12:20 pm. Coming down the Cajon Pass was great. Mileage at Rialto was 52726. Traveled 2825 miles from home.

After 16 days, they had finally reached their destination!

BOULDER CITY TO RIALTO AND HOME 2017 (2 DAYS)

We were now into the home stretch, just like Mom and Grandpa had been 83 years before. The pull to our destination was getting stronger and stronger. The difference is that we would end up at home whereas Mom and Grandpa would end up at Uncle Joe's house. In order to allow more time for stops, we had decided to split this part into two days.

Our first day saw us leaving Boulder City. While we were there, we discovered it was about the only place in Nevada where gambling, drinking and prostitution were illegal. Even though the rest of Nevada has seen fit to legalize these "indoor sports," Boulder City has not. We were told it's because all those things were prohibited during the dam building times when Boulder City was under Federal ownership. When the dam was finished and the town was turned over to the residents, the citizens voted then to keep the town as it was, and have done so ever since.

We also had to traverse the route Mom and Grandpa did; Boulder City, Mountain Pass and Cajon Pass. Coming down I-15, we noticed that other drivers were more impatient than they were in, say, Oklahoma or New Mexico on I-40. We were grateful for the lane reserved on the right for slow-moving vehicles. That usually meant the semis, since they had a lower speed limit than cars, but it also applied to Betsy with her top speed of 50. On some of the downhills, we did whiz along at up to 55, but that was not a sustainable speed.

The Mother Road Museum

Coming down Interstate 15 from Boulder City was not the most exciting road, but it is efficient. We found ourselves in Barstow in short order where one of our best finds was the Mother Road Museum. We met Debra and Ken Hodkin, volunteers who were most gracious in telling us about the museum.

Ken was even kind enough to take Betsy's picture on Route 66.

Betsy on Old Route 66

Leaving the Museum, we were really on the home stretch to Rialto and home. I knew my Uncle Joe lived there, but I had never found his address. Thanks to Google maps, I found a Van

Van Koevering Street in Rialto

Koevering Street in town! I don't know if he ever lived on that street, but I had to take this picture as the final souvenir of our trip.

We had made it 2953 miles; very close to Mom and Grandpa's 2825. We too had An Ordinary Adventure.

PART THREE
EPILOGUE

Our last stretch brought us into our own driveway. Home at last! Betsy heaved a sigh of relief as she pulled into the garage and Gerald shut off the motor.

But how did Mom and Grandpa get home? A small note near the end of Mom's notebook was in Grandpa's handwriting

11-21-34 arrived at Martin's home

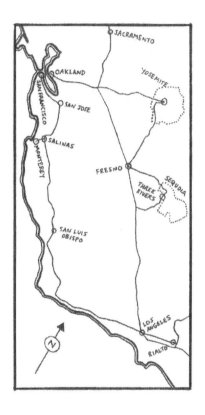

From November 12 to 21, they had stayed at Uncle Joe's home in Rialto and then moved to Uncle Martin's home. I had always thought he lived in Pasadena, but realized as I read the notebook further he lived in Glendale. But even from Uncle Martin's, I saw that Mom and Grandpa didn't just turn around and head home. Their Ordinary Adventure was going to continue with a trip to San Francisco via Sequoia and Yosemite! It seems getting home was going to be delayed for quite a while.

It wasn't until December 3 that they set out for San Francisco.

Saw lots of cotton fields, also snow covered mountains at the same time. Mountains are absolutely beautiful. Rented a cabin at Three Rivers near the Giant Forest. <u>Very</u> cold at night.

This route today would take them up the old Ridge Route over the San Gabriel Mountains at Tejon Pass, elevation 4144 feet, and then down into the central valley to Bakersfield. From there, they probably took what is now CA 65 and thus up the winding road to Three Rivers.

After visiting the Giant Forest,

Climbed in second gear for 18 miles to a height of 6400 feet. The Giant Trees are wonderful. Saw several deer and took pictures of some. Got within 4 feet of one. Eight inches of snow in the Giant Forest. Got stuck in the snow today. Very winding road leading to it. Mail boxes are made like bird houses.

When I read this part of Mom's notebook, it hit me that she mentioned taking a picture of some deer. This is the first and only mention of a camera, perhaps borrowed from Uncle Martin. But what happened to those pictures, I will sadly never know.

They finished this day by driving to Mariposa, outside of Yosemite, where they spent the night. The next morning,

Went to Yosemite National Park. Drove through the tunnel which is 8/10 miles long. Also drove all through the Valley and saw many beautiful rocks, falls, etc. Went on to Oakland where we rented a cabin. Much warmer here than where we spend the two preceding nights.

The Valley of the Yosemite

Those of us fortunate enough to have entered Yosemite from the south entrance will never cease to be thrilled by the trip through the tunnel. At first dark, with no hint of what is to come, soon the light at the end of the tunnel expands into the breathtaking view of one of the most beautiful places on earth; the Valley of the Yosemite.

We did not retrace this part of Mom and Grandpa's trip because it wasn't on Route 66, but we have visited both Sequoia and Yosemite National Parks in the past. But not with Betsy. Do I sense another Model A trip in the future?

Mom and Grandpa left Oakland the next morning and took a ferry to San Francisco and then took another ferry to Sausalito. If you're wondering why they didn't just take the San Francisco-Oakland Bay Bridge and the Golden Gate, those spans weren't there yet. Even though ground was broken for the Golden Gate on January 5, 1933, it wasn't open for traffic until May 27, 1937 and the Bay Bridge didn't open until 1936.

Just as at Boulder Dam, Mom and Grandpa were viewing an engineering marvel under construction – The Golden Gate Bridge. Their view from the ferry must have been quite good. Too bad they missed the grand opening: At noon on May 28, President Roosevelt pressed a telegraph key in the White House and announced the bridge's opening to the entire world. At 3 p.m. a fleet of 42 Navy ships sailed under the bridge and the day ended with a fireworks display at 10 p.m.

The Golden Gate Bridge

As for the Bay Bridge, it was a companion of the Golden Gate, but it has never engendered the same kind of interest and fame as its better-known companion. Construction began on July 9, 1933 and the opening was July 12, 1936, so once again, Mom and Grandpa missed the festivities.

The San Francisco-Oakland Bay Bridge

Since this was only a 5-day trip, they didn't spend much time in any one location.

Took a toll road down to Muir Woods which contain some very tall redwood trees. They are very beautiful. Took the ferry to San Francisco and then drove down to Colma where we visited some relatives. Saw Stanford University at Palo Alto.

I must pause here for a tongue-in-cheek question about "drove down to Colma where we visited some relatives."

Colma became the site for numerous cemeteries after San Francisco banned new interments within city limits in 1900 and then ousted all existing cemeteries in 1912. Approximately 150,000 bodies were moved between 1920 and 1941 at a cost of $10 apiece. The town of Colma itself only had about 1500 residents. So what did Mom really mean when she said they went to Colma and visited some relatives? Were they alive - or dead?

They stopped for the night in San Jose and then continued on to Monterey and over to Salinas.

Saw the California Polytechnic School at San Luis Obispo. Uncle Martin attended school there.

When I first thought about retracing Mom and Grandpa's Route 66 trip, I wondered why Uncle Joe and Uncle Martin were in California in the first place. That was a long way from Michigan. The answer came in the summer before our trip from an unlikely source – my brother Keith's son, Mark. Keith and Mark and his family live near Saratoga Springs, New York. Mark had saved some of the Van Koevering family history, so when I went to visit Keith for his birthday the previous June, I asked to see what Mark had saved. Out came the box with things I had never seen before. Since I was staying with Mark and his wife, Becca, I was in a perfect situation to rummage around in all this old stuff.

Mark set me up with the box and a copy machine and went off to work. I found an old family genealogy which had information dating back to 1650! What also amazed me was that this genealogy had been compiled by my mother's first cousin, Antoinette Van Koevering and typed up on a manual typewriter in 1982. Antoinette (Aunt Toni as we called her) was the daughter of my great-uncle Adrian (Uncle Ed from Zeeland Record fame). As you may recall, we had visited the Zeeland Record, now operated by my third cousin Kurt Van Koevering.

What made this genealogy so special was that Aunt Toni had not only laboriously typed up everyone's name, birth and death dates, marriage dates, and professions, but she had asked one of the surviving children to write some memories of their parents. And that's where I found the answer to my question of what brought my two great-uncles to California.

I found that Uncle Joe had tuberculosis and Uncle Martin had asthma (as did Grandpa). They were both advised to seek a milder climate under the care of a Dr Van Swalenberg in Riverside, California. They left Michigan in 1905 and never came back. They eventually recovered their health and stayed to find employment and raise families. Uncle Joe became an instructor in printing and Uncle Martin a geological engineer.

In 1975, during one of her Christmas visits to our home in California, Mom evidently visited Uncle Martin, because she saved a letter he wrote to her, dated December 23.

Dear Viola, It was so nice to hear from you and to recall the delightful visit you paid us. Do come again. Thank you very much for the family statistics...Lots of love, Martin

In one of the family rosters, someone made a handwritten entry that Uncle Martin's date of death was December 19, 1976, so she visited him just a year before he passed on at the age of 88. There was no visit to Uncle Joe because he passed on in 1953, at age 69.

Back row - William (1876-1917), Johannes Anthony (1883-1953) and Adrian (1874-1960);
Middle row - John (1871-1953), Isaac (1867-1952) and Christopher (1879-1958)
Front row - Martin (1888-1976) and Jennie (1881-1959)

Grandpa and His Siblings

As you can see from this picture, Jennie, the only daughter, was definitely outnumbered by her seven brothers. In the middle of the back row is Uncle Joe and on his left Uncle Ed. In the center middle row is Grandpa (love that moustache!) and the front row left is Uncle Martin. Grandpa was the oldest and Martin the youngest.

I find it interesting that of the seven brothers, their ages at death were 88, 86, 85, 81, 79, 69 and 40. Evidently the hard work they had to do growing up in the late 19th century resulted in a long life for five of the seven.

Meanwhile, in Mom's sparse writing, she tells us,

Left Santa Maria at 8:10 A.M. Came down San Marcos Pass in the rain. Plenty slippery. Arrived at Uncle Martin's in Glendale at 1:45 P.M. Mileage 54104. Traveled 1228 miles.

And all of that in just 5 days. That averages out to be about 245 miles per day. Having done our own Model A trip, I know that is a full day's drive. Considering a fair amount of the driving was over mountains and through valleys, I was impressed.

All the way throughout the trip from Grandville, Michigan to Rialto, California and from Uncle Martin's house in Glendale through Sequoia and Yosemite National Parks back to Glendale, Mom had kept up her journal and record of expenses. Grandpa also had kept up his habit of drawing the floor plans of every tourist cabin where they stayed. But there was one short entry on the last page of the Santa Maria floor plan in Grandpa's handwriting that was unexpected

Dec 12 – 1934 – 1:35 PM Glendale to Grandville
Viola left for home

These struck me as being very poignant words; his daughter and sole traveling companion was leaving for home without him! Mom did have to get back to work – and Bob, whom she hadn't seen in over seven weeks. She didn't keep a journal of her trip back because it wasn't very exciting. But what about Grandpa? He still had to get himself and the car home. When did he return and what route did he take?

Since Grandpa now had the notebook, he carried on what Mom had started; recording each day's mileage, leaving and arriving times, a weather report and anything of interest along the way.

On February 21, 1935, almost four months after leaving home, Grandpa left his brother Martin's home in Glendale to return to Joe's home in Rialto. If you have a really good memory, you might remember that the out-of-state permit they acquired in Yermo expired on December 31, 1934. Evidently, Grandpa had gotten it extended so he could continue his visit.

He and Joe spent a few days seeing the sights and just hanging out. Since Grandpa never visited California again, it was the last time we know of that he would see either of these two brothers.

2-22-35 We attended the national orange show at Sanbardino (San Bernardino) the show was very good

***2-23-35** raining in the forenoon and nice sunshine in the afternoon. Had oil changed in the crankcase and the brakes adjusted.*

***2-24-35** We took a drive to Riverside, Colton, Redlands and San Barnardino*

***2-25-35 54493** Started for home at 8 A.M.*

This was his itinerary:

Date	Route	Miles
Feb 25	Rialto CA to Gila Bend AZ	343
Feb 26	Gila Bend to Deming NM	382
Feb 27	Deming to Toyah TX	309
Feb 28	Toyah to Cisco TX	316
Mar 1	Cisco to Sulphur Springs TX	242
Mar 2	Sulphur Springs to Forrest City AR	356
Mar 3	Forrest City to Evansville IN	375
Mar 4	Evansville to Grandville MI	444
	Total Miles	**2767**

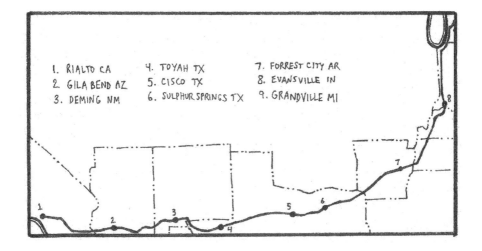

1. RIALTO CA   4. TOYAH TX   7. FORREST CITY AR
2. GILA BEND AZ   5. CISCO TX   8. EVANSVILLE IN
3. DEMING NM   6. SULPHUR SPRINGS TX   9. GRANDVILLE MI

After leaving Redlands it is mostly desert country. About 15 miles out it started and all day till I came near Gila Bend when an occasional farm came in sight in the east end of the Imperial Valley.

This was the same Imperial Valley that had been flooded by the Colorado River in the early 1900's and led to the eventual construction of Boulder Dam. It was obvious from the notebook that Grandpa was taking the southern route home. Route 66 would have been in the throes of winter and not a good choice. So instead of snowdrifts, Grandpa had sand drifts.

I saw large sand dunes. There was a very strong wind and the sand was piled in ridges on the pavement and sand roved like snow sometimes does across the pavement.

There is a two lane pavement across these sand dunes and with that strong wind it made it rather hard to stay on it. Once off it in that sand no telling when you would ever get out.

State inspection station at Yuma. Also set watch ahead one hour to Mountain Time. Arrived at Gila Bend at 5-30 PM

Fortunately, Grandpa didn't have to navigate over the old Plank Road that was built across the desert in the Imperial Valley in 1915. In 1926, the planks were replaced with pavement – what Grandpa was referring to here.

The Old Plank Road

One thing I noticed when I read over Grandpa's entries is that he left a lot sooner in the mornings than he and Mom had on the westward journey. The two of them would often not leave until close to 9 am, but

Grandpa's entries show him leaving usually between 7 and 7:30 am. I discovered he dispensed with cooking in the cabins and just got on the road. He had to do all the driving, so he couldn't eat and drive at the same time. In his meticulous record of expenses, it seems he bought breakfast, lunch and supper along the way each day.

Since he was driving alone, I think Grandpa just wanted to get home. As you can see from his itinerary, he made the return trip in eight days and he drove 2767 miles. That's averaging 346 miles a day! We never made that many daily miles on our trip, even when we weren't stopping to see anything.

Leaving Gila Bend in Arizona, the next stop was Deming, New Mexico. Just west of there is the Continental Divide, elevation 4585 feet. So Grandpa's Model A would have had to chug a bit to get over that hump. Today, it's all nicely paved Interstate 10, but not then.

...after leaving Phoenix I crossed three mountain passes 26 mi altogether with small valleys between. I saw two villages of wigwams. It was up and down hill nearly all day and desert, desert and some more desert. Arrived at Deming 5-15 PM

Between Deming and his next stop, El Paso, he **had the fan repacked and new brushes on Generator.** He arrived safely at the next burg, Toyah, at 5:40 pm. I had never heard of Toyah. When I looked it up on the map, I found it was over 200 miles east of El Paso, but not as far as Pecos. It was one of his shorter days.

Further traveling brought him through Odessa and Midland – oil country.

142

Old Oil Tanks

At Pyote there were at least 75 crude oil tanks for storage with wells scattered all around till near Odessa. Then at Midland there were a lot more tanks but no wells could be seen...arrived at Cisco at 6 PM

I could see that Grandpa wasn't staying in the bigger cities; he probably thought it would be too expensive. Cisco is a small burg east of Abilene and west of Fort Worth. He mentions pavement for the first time:

Had brick pavement nearly all the way from Cisco to Fort Worth.

He doesn't mention what the rest of the road surfaces were like, but judging from what Route 66 was like, they could have been dirt, gravel, asphalt, macadam or concrete.

His next stop was Sulphur Springs, east of Dallas but still in Texas. This was his third night in Texas and he was not out of it yet! Having driven across Texas many years ago, I can testify that it seems like Texas will go on forever. Leaving Sulphur Springs, he headed into Arkansas and stayed in Forrest City. What he found noteworthy was

The scenery very beautiful very much like Michigan...for about ten miles I saw nothing but Negroes...near Simms I also crossed a long bridge...it was a wooden structure near a mile long and as strait as a line

143

Like a horse heading for the barn, Grandpa was really picking up speed and making tracks for home; Forrest City, Arkansas to Evansville, Indiana and onward.

Came through Michigan City at about 5 P.M. decided to make home...took U.S. 12 to Benton Harbor then 12 to Kalamazoo then 131 to Grand Rapids and to Arthur's home but found them quarantined so went to Earl's home and stayed there a couple of days till I could arrange things to live at home. Arrived at Art's home at 9 P.M.

Earl and Art were two of Mom's older brothers and Grandpa was welcome to stay with either one except for the quarantine. What were they quarantined for?

In the early 1930's, Pearl Kendrick and Grace Eldering, who both received Doctor of Science degrees from Johns Hopkins University, were conducting original research into an effective vaccine for pertussis (whooping cough), which was highly contagious, especially among children. In the prior decade, about 6,000 children died from the disease each year. They were sponsored by the Michigan Department of Health, working in a laboratory located in Grand Rapids.

As part of their research, they discovered that most children were noninfectious by four weeks. Because of this, a method of quarantine was set up in Grand Rapids that would keep anyone who was infected at home and thus keep the disease from spreading. The quarantine period was 35 days. So Grandpa definitely wouldn't have wanted to stay at Art's home.

Fortunately, he could stay at Earl's house and arrange to have the utilities turned on at home so the house would be livable. But Mom had left California on December 12. It was now March 4. How did she get home? Why wasn't she living in the house? Where was she?

Mom did indeed leave California on December 12, 1934. And she did it in a Greyhound bus. She had left the precious notebook with Grandpa and evidently didn't care to get another one. After all, what could be exciting about a Greyhound bus ride? As a passenger, you have no control over the route you will be taking or what stops will be made.

Greyhound Bus Circa 1934

Many years later, when Mom was in her eighties, she would recount her most vivid memory of that cross-country ordeal – the lack of on-board restrooms, which weren't added to the buses until 1954. At the pre-arranged stops for restroom purposes, all the passengers had to be off and back on the bus in 15 minutes! Mom never said how many passengers there were or how many stalls, as this would have changed every time they came to a new stop. But she firmly remembered the 15-minute rule. As a result of the hurry-up situation, she said she became seriously constipated. Not exactly the kind of vivid memory anyone wants to have.

She didn't say how many days she had to endure this, but I'm sure it felt like far too many. When she finally arrived in Grandville, she wasn't in a position to open up the house and get the utilities turned on. Evidently, there was no need for her to be living alone in that big house so she would wait until Grandpa got back.

The arrangement for her return was for her to stay at her brother Art's house. That worked out fine until one day she returned from work and Art's wife Lila told Mom to get her clothes out right away. Their son had some communicable disease (probably whooping cough) and they were going to be quarantined. If she had stayed, she might have gotten the disease herself and, in any case, would not have been able to leave the house to go to work. Since they were still under quarantine when Grandpa got there in early March, the whooping cough may have been going around the family and the quarantine was extended.

She called her brother Earl and found his mother-in-law was staying there so there was no bed for her. Now what to do? Her two sisters lived too far away for her to stay with them and get to her job.

As a last option, she called her sweetie, Bob. His mother, Lottie, insisted that Mom come and stay with her, Bob and his younger brother, Jim. There were two extra bedrooms, so there was plenty of room for her.

Mom and Bob (my Dad) had met in high school and he used to walk her home from school long before they started dating. Their relationship grew over the years, through high school and her time in Business College. They were getting more serious and actually got engaged, but their mothers were not on speaking terms and they could never find out why. Mom decided a relationship under those circumstances wasn't going to work so she broke off the engagement. But when Mom's mother died that summer of 1934, that impediment to their relationship was gone. The door was now open.

When Grandpa finally returned in March, he opened up their house so he and Mom could move back in. In an account she wrote many years later for me and my brother Keith, here's how Mom described what happened next when she was leaving Bob's house to return to her own:

When I returned home, your Dad said to me, "Don't ever leave me again", and I didn't.

We were married that summer, and lived happily ever after.

When our trip was first taking shape, the idea of writing a book about it was not foremost in my mind. I'm not sure it was even in my mind at all.

But somewhere along the line, perhaps in the fall of 2016, the idea took hold. But what did I know about writing a book? I've written many term papers and a Master's thesis and essays and even taught essay-writing to high school juniors, but writing a book is a different matter.

I thought of Mike Rounds, whom I had met a few years back. He is a self-styled "book shepherd" and has helped about 2400 books see the light of day, either through direct coaching or his community college classes. Once he was on board, I felt more confident that my book would also see the light of day.

I didn't just want to write about "we went there, we did that and saw this" kind of book. I felt the desire to make this book a tribute to my mother, whom I dearly miss fifteen years after her passing.

The reason I titled this book An Ordinary Adventure is not because Mom and Grandpa's trip was ordinary. It certainly wasn't. But Mom and Grandpa were ordinary people in many ways. They were never rich or famous by any standards. They were decent, law-abiding citizens who grew up, went to school, got married, raised children, went to church, earned a living and paid their taxes.

Because of this ordinary life, I wanted to memorialize my mother and in that way, continue the relationship we had for sixty years and share her story with you.

So this book is my tribute to Mom; I know she is having a great time singing alto in the heavenly choir and maybe having even more Ordinary Adventures.

ACKNOWLEDGEMENTS

Kudos to Mike Rounds, my book shepherd. I had never written a book before and didn't know where to start. I first met Mike at Cerritos College where he taught an evening class, Self-Publishing for the Clueless®. I figured rather than trying to learn everything I might need to know to accomplish this project, it would be better to hire the brains and experience to get the job done. Thanks, Mike!

Leslie Sears is a graphic artist and Photoshop expert par excellence! There are so many things to get right in putting a book together and Leslie has done the cover and graphics proud.

My son Brendan devoted many hours to making the text flow. I figured if he could complete a 200-page dissertation, he knew something about writing. He became my official copy editor. He also inherited some artistic talent from his grandma and drew all the maps in each chapter so you'd know where we were.

Writers always save the best 'til last, and that honor goes to my Chief Car Guy, Chauffeur, Personal Mechanic and First Mate, Gerald. He did such an admirable job of driving, clutching the steering wheel for dear life and keeping his eyes glued to the road that I'm sure he's in line for a medal of some sort. I literally could not have done the trip without him since I still don't know how to drive the car!

If you enjoyed traveling with us on our **Ordinary Adventure,** please scan the QR code above.

It will take you to my website

www.LifeinTheDash.com

where you'll learn more about how I can help you live your best **Life In The Dash** - a life of passion and purpose, health, love and joy.

Thanks for joining the Life in the Dash community